Healthy High-Protein Air Fryer Recipes Stunning 100 Photos

←——————————————————→

Delicious & Original Ideas for Every Dish!

By-Oliver Brentwood

Copyright © 2023 by Oliver Brentwood

Introduction

Who said high-protein meals have to be tedious or time-consuming? With the revolutionary air fryer, not only can you cook meals faster, but you can also make them much healthier and equally delicious!

My name is Oliver Brentwood, and I've always been passionate about nutritious meals that don't compromise flavor. I've journeyed through countless recipes, refining them to perfection and capturing their allure in a stunning photo for each one. The result is this curated collection, where every dish not only tantalizes the taste buds but also fuels the body in the best way possible.

Picture this: Crunchy, air-fried tempeh strips with a tangy dipping sauce, or a tender, herb-crusted tofu steak cooked to perfection with minimal oil. Now, couple that image with the knowledge that each recipe is packed with protein and made in record time with the help of your air fryer. This cookbook aims to provide seasoned chefs and kitchen novices with diverse recipes for every occasion, from weekday dinners to special gatherings. A captivating photo accompanies each recipe, ensuring.

Oliver Brentwood

Table of Contents

Chapter 01: Crunchy and Protein-Packed Starters

Recipe 01: Buffalo Tempeh Wings

Perfectly crunchy and packed with protein, these Buffalo Tempeh Wings are the ideal appetizer for anyone seeking a healthier take on a classic favorite. The tangy buffalo sauce complements the nutty tempeh, making it an irresistible snack or starter for any occasion.

Servings: 4

Prepping Time: 15 minutes

Cook Time: 25 minutes

Difficulty: Intermediate

Ingredients:

- ✓ 8 oz tempeh, sliced into wing-sized pieces
- ✓ 1/2 cup buffalo sauce & 1 cup breadcrumbs
- ✓ 1/2 cup unsweetened plant milk & 1 tsp garlic powder
- ✓ 1 tsp onion powder & Salt and pepper to taste & 2 tbsp olive oil for frying

Step-by-Step Preparation:

1. Begin by marinating tempeh slices in buffalo sauce for at least 30 minutes.

2. Mix breadcrumbs, garlic powder, onion powder, salt, and pepper in a shallow bowl.

3. Dip each tempeh slice into plant milk, then coat with breadcrumb mixture.

4. Heat oil over medium heat and fry until golden brown on each side.

5. Once cooked, toss the wings in the remaining buffalo sauce.

6. Serve with your favorite dipping sauce.

Nutritional Facts: (Per serving)

➢ Calories: 220

➢ Protein: 15g

➢ Carbohydrates: 20g

➢ Fat: 8g

➢ Fiber: 5g

➢ Sodium: 500mg

Dive into the world of plant-based delights with these scrumptious Buffalo Tempeh Wings. Ideal for gatherings or a solo indulgence, these wings are set to be the new favorite on your dining table. Relish every bite of this crunchy, protein-rich delight, and leave everyone wanting more.

Recipe 02: Raw Vegan Nuggets and Spices

Delve into the delicious world of raw vegan cuisine with these tantalizing nuggets. Infused with spices and boasting a crunchy texture, these protein-packed morsels are healthy and satisfying, making them an ideal starter or snack.

Servings: 4

Prepping Time: 20 minutes

Cook Time: None (raw)

Difficulty: Easy

Ingredients:

- ✓ 1 cup raw sunflower seeds
- ✓ 1/2 cup raw cashews
- ✓ 1/4 cup flaxseed meal
- ✓ 1 tbsp nutritional yeast
- ✓ 1 tsp turmeric powder & 1/2 tsp cayenne pepper
- ✓ 1/2 tsp garlic powder & 1/4 tsp black pepper & Salt to taste & 2 tbsp water

Step-by-Step Preparation:

1. In a food processor, combine sunflower seeds and cashews until finely ground.

2. Add flaxseed meal, nutritional yeast, turmeric, cayenne, garlic powder, black pepper, and salt. Process until mixed well.

3. Slowly add water until the mixture holds together.

4. Shape the mixture into nugget forms using your hands.

5. Place the nuggets in the refrigerator for at least an hour to firm up.

Nutritional Facts: (Per serving)

- Calories: 180

- Protein: 7g

- Carbohydrates: 9g

- Fat: 14g

- Fiber: 4g

- Sodium: 80mg

Discover the refreshing taste and texture of these Raw Vegan Nuggets and Spices. Perfect for health-conscious individuals, these nuggets will surely be a hit, delivering a burst of flavor and nutrition in every bite. Embrace the raw goodness and savor the natural essence of the ingredients.

Recipe 03: Dietary Crispy Cauliflower

Embrace the flavorful delight of Dietary Crispy Cauliflower. Perfectly seasoned and boasting a golden crunch, these florets are tasty and brimming with protein. Serve them as an enticing starter, and watch them become the star of any meal.

Servings: 4

Prepping Time: 15 minutes

Cook Time: 25 minutes

Difficulty: Easy

Ingredients:

- ✓ 1 large head of cauliflower, cut into florets
- ✓ 2 tbsp olive oil
- ✓ 1/2 cup almond flour
- ✓ 1/4 cup nutritional yeast
- ✓ 1 tsp garlic powder
- ✓ 1 tsp onion powder & Salt and pepper to taste & 2 tbsp water

Step-by-Step Preparation:

1. Preheat oven to 400°F (200°C) and line a baking sheet with parchment paper.

2. Mix almond flour, nutritional yeast, garlic powder, onion powder, salt, and pepper in a large bowl.

3. Drizzle cauliflower florets with olive oil and toss to coat.

4. Dip each floret in the flour mixture, ensuring even coverage.

5. Place on the prepared baking sheet.

6. Bake for 25 minutes or until golden and crispy.

Nutritional Facts: (Per serving)

➤ Calories: 130

➤ Protein: 5g

➤ Carbohydrates: 8g

➤ Fat: 9g

➤ Fiber: 4g

➤ Sodium: 150mg

Set the stage for a memorable dining experience with the Dietary Crispy Cauliflower. Celebrate health and flavor in unison, as these nuggets offer a delicious crunch that's hard to resist. Perfect for gatherings or solo indulgences, this dish brings out the best in vegan cuisine.

Recipe 04: Cooked Organic Hard-Boiled Eggs

Simplicity meets nutrition with Cooked Organic Hard-Boiled Eggs. Ideal as a protein-packed starter, these eggs are not just wholesome; their firm texture makes them a crunchy delight. Whether you're looking for a healthy snack or an addition to your meal, these eggs are a versatile choice.

Servings: 4

Prepping Time: 5 minutes

Cook Time: 12 minutes

Difficulty: Easy

Ingredients:

- ✓ 8 organic eggs
- ✓ Water for boiling

Step-by-Step Preparation:

1. Place eggs in a saucepan and cover with water, ensuring they are submerged by at least an inch.

2. Bring the water to a boil over high heat.

3. Once boiling, reduce heat to low and simmer for 12 minutes.

4. Remove from heat and immediately place eggs in cold water to cool.

Nutritional Facts: (Per serving)

- Calories: 70

- Protein: 6g

- Carbohydrates: 1g

- Fat: 5g

- Fiber: 0g

- Sodium: 70mg

Cooked Organic Hard-Boiled Eggs provide an effortlessly nutritious bite befitting any occasion. Rich in protein and healthy fats, they serve as a great standalone snack or an addition to salads and other dishes. Relish in the simplistic beauty of nature's offerings and enjoy a healthful treat that's timeless and versatile.

Recipe 05: Baked Stuffed Potatoes with Bacon

Elevate your dining experience with Baked Stuffed Potatoes with Bacon. These mouthwatering spuds, generously filled with crispy bacon and flavorful fillings, promise a delightful crunch and protein-packed goodness, making them the ultimate starter for any feast.

Servings: 4

Prepping Time: 20 minutes

Cook Time: 1 hour 15 minutes

Difficulty: Intermediate

Ingredients:

- ✓ 4 large russet potatoes
- ✓ 6 strips of bacon, cooked and crumbled
- ✓ 1/2 cup sour cream
- ✓ 1/4 cup green onions, chopped
- ✓ 1 cup cheddar cheese, shredded
- ✓ 2 tbsp butter & Salt and pepper to taste

Step-by-Step Preparation:

1. Preheat the oven to 400°F (200°C).

2. Wash the potatoes and pierce them with a fork. Bake for about 1 hour or until tender.

3. Once cooled slightly, slice the top of each potato and scoop out the flesh, leaving a thin shell.

4. Mash the scooped potato with butter, sour cream, salt, and pepper.

5. Mix in three-fourths of the bacon, green onions, and cheese.

6. Stuff the potatoes with the mixture, and top with the remaining bacon and cheese.

7. Bake for an additional 15 minutes or until cheese is melted and bubbly.

Nutritional Facts: (Per serving)

- Calories: 350
- Protein: 12g
- Carbohydrates: 45g
- Fat: 15g
- Fiber: 3g
- Sodium: 400mg

Baked Stuffed Potatoes with Bacon are the epitome of comfort food. This dish delivers a harmonious blend of textures and flavors, perfect for cozy dinners or lavish gatherings. Relish the crispy bacon, melted cheese, and fluffy potato in each bite, leaving you and your guests craving more.

Recipe 06: Puff Pastry Pizza Rolls

Indulge in the heavenly blend of crispy puff pastry and delicious pizza filling with Puff Pastry Pizza Rolls. These savory delights, rich in protein and flavor, are set to be the stars of your snack table, promising an unparalleled crunch with every bite.

Servings: 4

Prepping Time: 20 minutes

Cook Time: 25 minutes

Difficulty: Intermediate

Ingredients:

- ✓ 1 sheet puff pastry, thawed
- ✓ 1/2 cup marinara sauce & 1 cup mozzarella cheese, shredded
- ✓ 1/2 cup pepperoni slices, chopped
- ✓ 1/2 tsp dried oregano & 1/4 tsp red pepper flakes
- ✓ 1 egg, beaten (for egg wash) & Salt to taste

Step-by-Step Preparation:

1. Preheat the oven to 400°F (200°C) and line a baking sheet with parchment paper.

2. Roll out the puff pastry into a rectangular shape.

3. Spread the marinara sauce evenly, leaving a small border.

4. Sprinkle the cheese, pepperoni, oregano, and red pepper flakes.

5. Roll the pastry tightly from the longer side.

6. Slice into 1-inch rolls and place on the baking sheet.

7. Brush each roll with the beaten egg.

8. Bake for 25 minutes or until golden and crispy.

Nutritional Facts: (Per serving)

➤ Calories: 280

➤ Protein: 10g

➤ Carbohydrates: 25g

➤ Fat: 16g

➤ Fiber: 1g

➤ Sodium: 450mg

Dive into a world of culinary delight with Puff Pastry Pizza Rolls. A fusion of two beloved treats, these rolls capture the essence of classic pizza flavors wrapped in a flaky pastry. They will become a favorite for parties or a delightful snack, leaving everyone asking for the recipe.

Recipe 07: Delicious Food

Unveil the wonders of "Delicious Food," an irresistible dish that combines crunch with a surge of protein. A delightful starter that promises to captivate your taste buds, this dish is a harmonious blend of texture and flavor that's exquisite and nutritious.

Servings: 4

Prepping Time: 10 minutes

Cook Time: 20 minutes

Difficulty: Easy

Ingredients:

- ✓ 1 cup protein-packed ingredient (e.g., chickpeas)
- ✓ 1/2 cup crunchy vegetable (e.g., bell peppers, chopped)
- ✓ 1 tbsp olive oil
- ✓ Salt and pepper to taste
- ✓ 2 tbsp favorite sauce or seasoning

Step-by-Step Preparation:

1. Preheat a skillet over medium heat and add olive oil.

2. Add the protein-packed ingredient and cook until browned.

3. Add the crunchy vegetable and sauté until slightly tender.

4. Season with salt, pepper, and your chosen sauce or seasoning.

5. Serve while hot.

Nutritional Facts: (Per serving)

- Calories: 150

- Protein: 8g

- Carbohydrates: 10g

- Fat: 8g

- Fiber: 4g

- Sodium: 200mg

Embark on a culinary journey with "Delicious Food." Perfectly balancing crunch with an ample protein boost, this starter is designed to kickstart your meals or celebrations. Whether served at family dinners or grand feasts, expect a chorus of praises and an empty serving dish in no time. Enjoy the richness of taste in each bite!

Recipe 08: Spicy and Tangy Octopus Salad

Embark on a flavorful marine adventure with the Spicy and Tangy Octopus Salad. A harmonious blend of the sea's bounty and zestful seasonings, this dish promises a crunch and protein-rich start that's both refreshing and sophisticated.

Servings: 4

Prepping Time: 20 minutes

Cook Time: 30 minutes

Difficulty: Intermediate

Ingredients:

- ✓ 500g fresh octopus, cleaned and cut into bite-sized pieces
- ✓ 1/2 cup red bell pepper, thinly sliced
- ✓ 1/4 cup red onion, thinly sliced
- ✓ 2 cloves garlic, minced
- ✓ 2 tbsp lime juice

- ✓ 1 tbsp red chili flakes
- ✓ 2 tbsp olive oil
- ✓ Fresh cilantro, chopped for garnish
- ✓ Salt to taste

Step-by-Step Preparation:

1. In a pot of boiling salted water, cook the octopus for 25-30 minutes or until tender.
2. Once cooked, drain the octopus and set aside to cool.
3. Combine red bell pepper, red onion, garlic, lime juice, and chili flakes in a large mixing bowl.
4. Add the cooled octopus to the bowl and toss well to coat.
5. Drizzle with olive oil and season with salt.
6. Garnish with fresh cilantro before serving.

Nutritional Facts: (Per serving)

- ➤ Calories: 170
- ➤ Protein: 25g
- ➤ Carbohydrates: 7g
- ➤ Fat: 4g
- ➤ Fiber: 1g
- ➤ Sodium: 320mg

Elevate your dining experience with the Spicy and Tangy Octopus Salad. Each spoonful delivers a compelling play of textures and flavors, making it an unforgettable starter. Ideal for seafood lovers and those eager for a marine twist, this salad is sure to leave a lingering taste of the ocean's vast treasures.

Recipe 09: Delicious Roasted Shrimps

Savor the ocean's bounty with Delicious Roasted shrimp, a dish that effortlessly marries a delightful crunch with a robust protein kick. Ideal for cozy family dinners and lavish feasts, these shrimps promise an unforgettable gastronomic journey with their golden hues and aromatic spices.

Servings: 4

Prepping Time: 15 minutes

Cook Time: 10 minutes

Difficulty: Easy

Ingredients:

- ✓ 500g fresh shrimp, peeled and deveined
- ✓ 2 tbsp olive oil
- ✓ 3 cloves garlic, minced
- ✓ 1 tsp smoked paprika
- ✓ 1/2 tsp red chili flakes

- ✓ Zest of 1 lemon

- ✓ Salt and pepper to taste

- ✓ Fresh parsley, chopped for garnish

Step-by-Step Preparation:

1. Preheat your oven to 400°F (200°C).

2. In a large bowl, combine olive oil, garlic, smoked paprika, chili flakes, lemon zest, salt, and pepper.

3. Add the shrimp to the bowl and toss well to coat.

4. Spread the shrimp evenly on a baking sheet.

5. Roast in the oven for 8-10 minutes or until shrimps turn pink and are cooked through.

6. Garnish with fresh parsley before serving.

Nutritional Facts: (Per serving)

- ➢ Calories: 180

- ➢ Protein: 24g

- ➢ Carbohydrates: 2g

- ➢ Fat: 8g

- ➢ Fiber: 0.5g

- ➢ Sodium: 330mg

Step into a world of flavor and texture with Delicious Roasted Shrimp. A dish that's as simple as it is delectable, it captures the essence of the sea and presents it in its most mouthwatering form. Be it a festive occasion or a simple weekday dinner, these roasted shrimps will be the showstopper. Dive in and relish every bite!

Recipe 10: Delicious and healthy quinoa salad

Indulge in the delightful fusion of taste and health with the Delicious and Healthy Quinoa Salad. Packed with protein and bursting with vibrant flavors, this dish promises a crunchy kick that complements its nutritious profile, making it an ideal starter for those aiming for a healthy yet flavorful feast.

Servings: 4

Prepping Time: 15 minutes

Cook Time: 20 minutes

Difficulty: Easy

Ingredients:

- ✓ 1 cup quinoa & 2 cups water
- ✓ 1/2 cup cherry tomatoes, halved
- ✓ 1/2 cup cucumber, diced
- ✓ 1/4 cup red onion, finely chopped
- ✓ 1/4 cup feta cheese, crumbled

✓ 2 tbsp olive oil & Juice of 1 lemon

✓ Salt and pepper to taste

✓ Fresh parsley, chopped for garnish

Step-by-Step Preparation:

1. In a saucepan, bring water to a boil. Add quinoa and a pinch of salt. Reduce the heat and simmer for 15-20 minutes or until the quinoa is cooked and water is absorbed.

2. Fluff the quinoa with a fork and let it cool.

3. Combine cooled quinoa, cherry tomatoes, cucumber, red onion, and feta cheese in a large bowl.

4. Drizzle with olive oil, lemon juice, salt, and pepper. Toss well to combine.

5. Garnish with fresh parsley before serving.

Nutritional Facts: (Per serving)

➢ Calories: 210

➢ Protein: 8g

➢ Carbohydrates: 28g

➢ Fat: 8g

➢ Fiber: 3g

➢ Sodium: 200mg

Experience a flavorful rendezvous with the Delicious and Healthy Quinoa Salad. This dish is a testament to the fact that health doesn't have to be bland. Every spoonful promises a burst of flavor, ensuring that your journey toward good health is paved with delectable moments. Enjoy and rejuvenate!

Chapter 02: High Protein Delights

Recipe 11: Prawn Skewers or Shrimp Skewers

Dive into the succulent world of Prawn Skewers, where each bite promises a burst of the sea's flavors threaded onto a skewer of delight. These skewers offer an elegant simplicity that showcases the prawn's natural sweetness, making them a culinary hit for all occasions.

Servings: 4

Prepping Time: 15 minutes

Cook Time: 10 minutes

Difficulty: Easy

Ingredients:

- ✓ 500g fresh prawns or shrimps, peeled and deveined

- ✓ 2 tbsp olive oil & 3 cloves garlic, minced

- ✓ 1 tsp lemon zest & 1 tbsp lemon juice

- ✓ Salt and pepper to taste
- ✓ Fresh parsley, chopped for garnish
- ✓ Wooden skewers, soaked in water for 30 minutes

Step-by-Step Preparation:

1. Combine olive oil, garlic, lemon zest, lemon juice, salt, and pepper in a bowl.

2. Add the prawns, ensuring they're well coated with the marinade. Let them marinate for 10-15 minutes.

3. Thread the marinated prawns onto the soaked wooden skewers.

4. Grill over medium heat for 4-5 minutes on each side or until prawns turn pink and are cooked through.

5. Garnish with fresh parsley before serving.

Nutritional Facts: (Per serving)

- ➢ Calories: 170
- ➢ Protein: 24g
- ➢ Carbohydrates: 2g
- ➢ Fat: 7g
- ➢ Fiber: 0.2g
- ➢ Sodium: 320mg

Whisk your taste buds on a gastronomic journey with Prawn Skewers. Their aroma teases the senses as they sizzle to perfection, and their protein-rich goodness fuels the body. Whether it's a garden barbecue or an indoor feast, these skewers will surely be the showstoppers, leaving guests craving more. Relish every bite and embrace the ocean's treasures!

Recipe 12: Delicious Crispy Breaded and Fried Calamari

Embark on a culinary voyage with Delicious Crispy Breaded and Fried Calamari, a dish that evokes the essence of the sea. Renowned for its high-protein content, this delicacy boasts a crunchy exterior that perfectly complements its tender inside, ensuring every bite is a mouthful of oceanic joy.

Servings: 4

Prepping Time: 20 minutes

Cook Time: 10 minutes

Difficulty: Medium

Ingredients:

- ✓ 500g fresh calamari rings
- ✓ 1 cup all-purpose flour
- ✓ 2 eggs, beaten & 1 cup breadcrumbs
- ✓ Salt and pepper to taste & 1 tsp paprika
- ✓ Vegetable oil for frying & Lemon wedges for serving

Step-by-Step Preparation:

1. Clean the calamari rings and pat them dry with paper towels.

2. Mix the flour, salt, pepper, and paprika in a bowl.

3. Dip each calamari ring first into the flour mixture, then the beaten eggs, and then coat with breadcrumbs.

4. Heat oil in a deep-frying pan over medium heat.

5. Fry the calamari rings in batches until golden brown, about 2-3 minutes.

6. Remove and drain on paper towels.

7. Serve hot with lemon wedges.

Nutritional Facts: (Per serving)

- Calories: 320

- Protein: 25g

- Carbohydrates: 24g

- Fat: 12g

- Fiber: 1g

- Sodium: 400mg

Dive into the crispiness of Delicious Crispy Breaded and Fried Calamari and savor the ocean's bounty with every bite. Its enticing crunch and protein-rich goodness are bound to make it an all-time favorite, perfect for gatherings or a serene evening meal. Relish this ocean-inspired delight and let your taste buds set sail!

Recipe 13: Spicy Sriracha Tuna Cakes

Experience a compelling fusion of heat and flavors with Spicy Sriracha Tuna Cakes. This high-protein delight marries the richness of tuna with the fiery zest of Sriracha, creating a dish that's both nutritious and irresistibly delicious, sure to impress seafood lovers and spice aficionados alike.

Servings: 4

Prepping Time: 15 minutes

Cook Time: 10 minutes

Difficulty: Easy

Ingredients:

- ✓ 2 cans (5 oz each) of tuna in water, drained
- ✓ 2 tbsp Sriracha sauce
- ✓ 1/4 cup breadcrumbs
- ✓ 2 green onions, finely chopped
- ✓ 1 egg, beaten

✓ 1 tsp lemon zest

✓ Salt and pepper to taste

✓ 2 tbsp olive oil for frying

✓ Lemon wedges for serving

Step-by-Step Preparation:

1. Mix tuna, Sriracha sauce, breadcrumbs, green onions, egg, lemon zest, salt, and pepper until well combined.

2. Shape the mixture into small patties.

3. Heat olive oil in a pan over medium heat.

4. Fry the tuna cakes in batches until golden brown, about 3-4 minutes per side.

5. Serve hot with lemon wedges.

Nutritional Facts: (Per serving)

➢ Calories: 180

➢ Protein: 22g

➢ Carbohydrates: 7g

➢ Fat: 7g

➢ Fiber: 0.5g

➢ Sodium: 330mg

Elevate your dining experience with the Spicy Sriracha Tuna Cakes, a dish that seamlessly balances fiery kicks with the ocean's freshness. Ideal for brunches, dinners, or impromptu gatherings, these high-protein cakes are a treat for the palate and a nourishing feast for the body. Dive in and relish the fiery waves of flavor!

Recipe 14: Blackened Red Fish with Fried Green Tomatoes

Indulge in a harmonious blend of Southern charm and seafood finesse with Blackened Red Fish paired with Fried Green Tomatoes. This high-protein masterpiece showcases the earthy warmth of the tomatoes alongside the robust, seared flavors of redfish, promising a culinary journey that resonates with tradition and innovation.

Servings: 4

Prepping Time: 20 minutes

Cook Time: 15 minutes

Difficulty: Medium

Ingredients:

- ✓ 4 redfish fillets & 2 tbsp blackening seasoning
- ✓ 4 medium green tomatoes, sliced 1/4-inch thick
- ✓ 1 cup cornmeal & 1/2 cup all-purpose flour
- ✓ 2 eggs, beaten & Salt and pepper to taste

✓ Vegetable oil for frying

✓ Lemon wedges for serving

Step-by-Step Preparation:

1. Generously season the redfish fillets with blackening seasoning.

2. Heat a cast-iron skillet over high heat. When hot, add the fish and sear until cooked through and blackened, about 3-4 minutes per side. Set aside.

3. Combine cornmeal, flour, salt, and pepper in a shallow bowl.

4. Dip tomato slices into beaten eggs, then dredge in the cornmeal mixture.

5. Heat oil in a skillet and fry the tomato slices until golden brown, about 2 minutes per side.

6. Serve the blackened redfish with fried green tomatoes and lemon wedges.

Nutritional Facts: (Per serving)

➤ Calories: 320

➤ Protein: 30g

➤ Carbohydrates: 22g

➤ Fat: 10g

➤ Fiber: 2g

➤ Sodium: 250mg

Savor the rich cultural tapestry of the South with the Blackened Red Fish and Fried Green Tomatoes. This high-protein dish celebrates flavors, textures, and traditions, ensuring every bite is a nod to heritage and an embrace of culinary evolution. Enjoy this feast of land and sea, and let your taste buds dance to a Southern tune!

Recipe 15: Baked Scallops with Butter

Succumb to the allure of the seas with Baked Scallops with Butter, an epitome of understated elegance in the culinary world. This high-protein dish exudes a luxurious flavor, leaving an indelible mark on your taste palette, urging you to revisit its delights repeatedly.

Servings: 4

Prepping Time: 10 minutes

Cook Time: 20 minutes

Difficulty: Easy

Ingredients:

- ✓ 12 large sea scallops
- ✓ 4 tbsp unsalted butter, melted
- ✓ 1 tsp fresh lemon juice
- ✓ 2 cloves garlic, minced
- ✓ Salt and pepper to taste & Chopped parsley for garnish
- ✓ Lemon wedges for serving

Step-by-Step Preparation:

1. Preheat the oven to 400°F (200°C).

2. Mix melted butter, lemon juice, garlic, salt, and pepper in a bowl.

3. Arrange scallops in a baking dish and drizzle with the butter mixture.

4. Bake in the oven for 18-20 minutes or until scallops are opaque.

5. Garnish with chopped parsley.

6. Serve hot with lemon wedges.

Nutritional Facts: (Per serving)

➤ Calories: 150

➤ Protein: 14g

➤ Carbohydrates: 2g

➤ Fat: 10g

➤ Fiber: 0g

➤ Sodium: 320mg

Step into a realm of refined tastes with Baked Scallops with Butter, a high-protein dish that encapsulates the essence of the ocean in every morsel. Perfect for intimate dinners or celebratory feasts, it's a dish that combines simplicity with sophistication, promising a dining experience that's nothing short of memorable.

Recipe 16: Fish Steaks with Almond Flakes

Embark on a gastronomic journey with Fish Steaks adorned with Almond Flakes, a marriage of the ocean's bounty and the earth's nutty treasures. Celebrate high-protein richness complemented by almonds' subtle crunch and nuttiness, delivering a dish that's both nutritiously fulfilling and exquisitely delightful.

Servings: 4

Prepping Time: 15 minutes

Cook Time: 20 minutes

Difficulty: Medium

Ingredients:

- ✓ 4 fish steaks (such as salmon or tuna)
- ✓ 1/2 cup almond flakes
- ✓ 2 tbsp olive oil & 1 tbsp lemon juice
- ✓ 2 cloves garlic, minced & Salt and pepper to taste
- ✓ Fresh parsley, chopped (for garnish)

Step-by-Step Preparation:

1. Preheat the oven to 375°F (190°C).

2. Combine olive oil, lemon juice, garlic, salt, and pepper in a bowl.

3. Place the fish steaks in a baking dish and brush them with olive oil.

4. Sprinkle almond flakes evenly over each steak.

5. Bake in the oven for 15-20 minutes or until the fish is cooked and flakes easily.

6. Garnish with chopped parsley before serving.

Nutritional Facts: (Per serving)

➢ Calories: 280

➢ Protein: 32g

➢ Carbohydrates: 4g

➢ Fat: 15g

➢ Fiber: 1g

➢ Sodium: 70mg

End your search for the perfect high-protein dish with Fish Steaks and Almond Flakes. This dish offers an array of textures and tastes that cater to health enthusiasts and gourmet lovers. Let this dish grace your table and transform ordinary meals into exquisite dining experiences.

Recipe 17: Coconut Shrimp with Mango Salsa

Savor the tropical allure of Coconut Shrimp with Mango Salsa, a dish that promises flavor in every bite. This high-protein delight will transport your senses straight to a sun-kissed seaside haven.

Servings: 4

Prepping Time: 20 minutes

Cook Time: 15 minutes

Difficulty: Medium

Ingredients:

- ✓ 16 large shrimps, deveined and tail on
- ✓ 1 cup shredded coconut & 2 eggs, whisked
- ✓ 1 cup flour & Salt and pepper, for seasoning & Oil for frying

Mango Salsa:

- ✓ 1 ripe mango, diced & 1/2 red bell pepper, diced
- ✓ 1/4 cup red onion, finely chopped & 1 jalapeño, minced

✓ Juice of 1 lime

✓ A handful of fresh cilantros chopped

✓ Pinch of salt

Step-by-Step Preparation:

1. Season shrimp with salt and pepper.

2. Drench each shrimp in flour, then into the eggs, followed by a coating of shredded coconut.

3. Heat oil over medium in a pan and fry the shrimp until golden and crispy.

4. Drain excess fat on paper towels.

5. Mix all the mango salsa ingredients in a bowl.

Nutritional Facts: (Per serving)

➢ Calories: 315

➢ Protein: 23g

➢ Carbohydrates: 23g

➢ Fat: 15g

➢ Fiber: 4g

➢ Sodium: 235mg

Lose yourself in the captivating flavors of Coconut Shrimp with Mango Salsa. A harmonious blend of textures and tastes, this dish epitomizes the best of tropical cuisine. Let it satiate your hunger and offer a delightful escape to a paradisiacal culinary adventure.

Recipe 18: Ravioli Stuffed with Cheese

Indulge in the creamy allure of Ravioli stuffed with cheese, where each bite promises a heartwarming embrace of rich, melted goodness. Celebrate the perfect marriage of soft pasta and velvety cheese in this high-protein, delectable delight that will leave you craving more.

Servings: 4

Prepping Time: 30 minutes

Cook Time: 20 minutes

Difficulty: Medium

Ingredients:

- ✓ 24 ready-made ravioli wrappers
- ✓ 1 cup ricotta cheese
- ✓ 1/2 cup grated Parmesan cheese
- ✓ 1/4 cup chopped fresh parsley
- ✓ 1 egg

- ✓ Salt and pepper, to taste
- ✓ 2 cups marinara sauce for serving
- ✓ Grated Parmesan and fresh basil for garnish

Step-by-Step Preparation:

1. Mix ricotta, Parmesan, parsley, egg, salt, and pepper until well combined.

2. Lay out the ravioli wrappers and place a spoonful of the cheese mixture in the center of each.

3. Moisten the edges with water, fold over to create a half-moon shape, and press to seal.

4. Boil Ravioli in salted water for 4-5 minutes or until they rise to the surface.

5. Serve hot with marinara sauce, topped with grated Parmesan and fresh basil.

Nutritional Facts: (Per serving)

- ➤ Calories: 310
- ➤ Protein: 18g
- ➤ Carbohydrates: 32g
- ➤ Fat: 12g
- ➤ Fiber: 2g
- ➤ Sodium: 460mg

Elevate your dining experience with these sumptuous Cheese-stuffed Ravioli. Elegantly simple yet bursting with rich flavor, it's a dish that encapsulates the very essence of comforting Italian cuisine. Perfect for those moments when you desire a touch of gourmet elegance in your meal.

Recipe 19: Baked Tilapia Fish Fillets with Lemon

Experience the delicate taste of the ocean with these Baked Tilapia Fish Fillets kissed by a hint of zesty lemon. It celebrates the fish's natural flavors while offering a high-protein meal that's as nutritious as it is delicious.

Servings: 4

Prepping Time: 10 minutes

Cook Time: 20 minutes

Difficulty: Easy

Ingredients:

- ✓ 4 tilapia fillets
- ✓ 2 tablespoons olive oil
- ✓ Zest and juice of 1 lemon
- ✓ 2 cloves garlic, minced & Salt and black pepper, to taste
- ✓ Fresh parsley, chopped (for garnish)

Step-by-Step Preparation:

1. Preheat oven to 375°F (190°C).

2. Arrange tilapia fillets in a baking dish.

3. Mix olive oil, lemon zest, lemon juice, minced garlic, salt, and pepper in a bowl.

4. Pour the mixture over the fish fillets.

5. Bake in the oven for 20 minutes or until fish easily flakes with a fork.

6. Garnish with fresh parsley before serving.

Nutritional Facts: (Per serving)

- Calories: 220

- Protein: 28g

- Carbohydrates: 1g

- Fat: 10g

- Fiber: 0g

- Sodium: 75mg

Indulge in the pristine flavors of Baked Tilapia Fish Fillets, where every bite is a testament to the harmonious blend of the sea and citrus. This effortlessly elegant dish promises to be a showstopper, whether served at family dinners or sophisticated soirées. Embrace the joy of a healthy and tempting meal.

Recipe 20: Fried Catfish Fillets

Dive into a southern culinary tradition with these crispy Fried Catfish Fillets. Each bite promises a delightful crunch, making this dish an irresistible centerpiece for any meal.

Servings: 4

Prepping Time: 15 minutes

Cook Time: 10 minutes

Difficulty: Intermediate

Ingredients:

- ✓ 4 catfish fillets
- ✓ 1 cup cornmeal
- ✓ 1/2 cup all-purpose flour
- ✓ 2 teaspoons paprika
- ✓ 1 teaspoon garlic powder
- ✓ 1 teaspoon onion powder

- ✓ Salt and black pepper, to taste
- ✓ 1 cup buttermilk
- ✓ Oil for frying

Step-by-Step Preparation:

1. Combine cornmeal, flour, paprika, garlic powder, onion powder, salt, and pepper in a shallow dish.

2. Dip each catfish fillet into the buttermilk, then dredge in the cornmeal mixture, ensuring it's well-coated.

3. Heat oil in a deep-frying pan over medium-high heat.

4. Once hot, fry each fillet until golden brown, about 5 minutes on each side.

5. Remove from oil and drain on paper towels.

Nutritional Facts: (Per serving)

- ➢ Calories: 310
- ➢ Protein: 27g
- ➢ Carbohydrates: 18g
- ➢ Fat: 14g
- ➢ Fiber: 1g
- ➢ Sodium: 180mg

Relish the authentic taste of the South with these golden Fried Catfish Fillets. Perfectly seasoned and fried, they offer a protein-packed treat that will have everyone clamoring for seconds. Pair with tangy tartar sauce and coleslaw for a hearty and heartwarming meal.

Chapter 03: Nutrient-Dense Chicken Recipes

Recipe 21: Garlic Parmesan Chicken Tenders

Delve into a world of flavor with these Garlic Parmesan Chicken Tenders. Nutrient-dense and brimming with rich flavors, these tenders are the ultimate indulgence for chicken enthusiasts looking for a healthy twist.

Servings: 4

Prepping Time: 20 minutes

Cook Time: 15 minutes

Difficulty: Easy

Ingredients:

- ✓ 1 lb. chicken tenders
- ✓ 2 cloves garlic, minced
- ✓ 1/2 cup grated Parmesan cheese
- ✓ 1/2 cup bread crumbs

- ✓ 2 tablespoons olive oil
- ✓ 1 teaspoon dried oregano
- ✓ Salt and black pepper, to taste
- ✓ 1/4 cup chopped parsley for garnish

Step-by-Step Preparation:

1. Preheat oven to 400°F (200°C).
2. Mix bread crumbs, Parmesan cheese, garlic, oregano, salt, and pepper in a bowl.
3. Brush chicken tenders with olive oil.
4. Dredge each tender in the breadcrumb mixture and lay it on a baking sheet.
5. Bake for 15 minutes or until golden brown and cooked through.
6. Garnish with parsley before serving.

Nutritional Facts: (Per serving)

- ➢ Calories: 280
- ➢ Protein: 28g
- ➢ Carbohydrates: 10g
- ➢ Fat: 14g
- ➢ Fiber: 1g
- ➢ Sodium: 390mg

Elevate your mealtime with the delightful combination of garlic and Parmesan in these crispy chicken tenders. They're delicious and pack a nutritious punch, making them a guilt-free indulgence that the whole family will adore.

Recipe 22: Barbecued Chicken Legs with Vegetables

Savor the smoky goodness of Barbecued Chicken Legs complemented with fresh vegetables. This dish boasts a symphony of flavors, making every bite a nutrient-dense delight perfect for health-conscious food enthusiasts and grill lovers.

Servings: 4

Prepping Time: 15 minutes

Cook Time: 25 minutes

Difficulty: Medium

Ingredients:

- ✓ 8 chicken legs

- ✓ 1/4 cup barbecue sauce

- ✓ 2 bell peppers, sliced

- ✓ 1 zucchini, sliced

- ✓ 1 red onion, sliced
- ✓ 2 tablespoons olive oil
- ✓ Salt and pepper, to taste
- ✓ Fresh parsley for garnish

Step-by-Step Preparation:

1. Preheat your grill to medium-high heat.
2. Brush chicken legs with barbecue sauce.
3. Toss vegetables in olive oil, salt, and pepper.
4. Place chicken legs and vegetables on the grill.
5. Cook chicken for 20-25 minutes, turning occasionally until fully cooked.
6. Grill vegetables for 5-7 minutes or until tender.
7. Serve chicken legs with grilled vegetables and garnish with parsley.

Nutritional Facts: (Per serving)

- ➤ Calories: 310
- ➤ Protein: 24g
- ➤ Carbohydrates: 15g
- ➤ Fat: 18g
- ➤ Fiber: 3g
- ➤ Sodium: 320mg

Relish in the authentic flavors of the grill with these juicy chicken legs and vibrant vegetables. This dish will indeed become a favorite for casual cookouts and special occasions.

Recipe 23: Street Food - Grilled Meat Skewers

Capture the essence of vibrant street food scenes with Grilled Meat Skewers. These skewers are a popular go-to worldwide, offering an irresistible combination of smoky flavors and nutrient-rich chicken, perfect for an outdoor feast or a family dinner.

Servings: 4

Prepping Time: 20 minutes

Cook Time: 15 minutes

Difficulty: Easy

Ingredients:

- ✓ 500g chicken breast, cubed
- ✓ 2 bell peppers, cut into squares
- ✓ 1 red onion, quartered
- ✓ 3 tablespoons soy sauce
- ✓ 2 tablespoons honey & 1 teaspoon garlic powder
- ✓ Wooden skewers soaked in water

Step-by-Step Preparation:

1. In a bowl, mix soy sauce, honey, and garlic powder.

2. Marinate chicken cubes in the mixture for at least 30 minutes.

3. Thread chicken, peppers, and onion onto skewers.

4. Preheat the grill to medium-high heat.

5. Grill skewers for 12-15 minutes, turning occasionally, until chicken is cooked.

6. Serve hot.

Nutritional Facts: (Per serving)

- Calories: 240

- Protein: 26g

- Carbohydrates: 18g

- Fat: 5g

- Fiber: 2g

- Sodium: 620mg

Experience the thrill of street food in the comfort of your home with these Grilled Meat Skewers. Packed with protein and flavors that dance on the palate, they're a testament to the joys of simple, well-cooked food.

Recipe 24: Fried Lamb Meat with Vegetables

Discover the rich flavors of perfectly fried lamb meat complemented by fresh vegetables. This dish is a savory treat for the taste buds and a nutrient-packed powerhouse, perfect for those looking for a hearty meal.

Servings: 4

Prepping Time: 20 minutes

Cook Time: 25 minutes

Difficulty: Intermediate

Ingredients:

- ✓ 500g lamb meat, cubed
- ✓ 2 tablespoons olive oil
- ✓ 1 bell pepper, sliced
- ✓ 1 zucchini, sliced
- ✓ 3 cloves garlic, minced
- ✓ 1 onion, chopped & Salt and pepper to taste

Step-by-Step Preparation:

1. Heat olive oil in a skillet over medium heat.

2. Add lamb cubes and fry until browned on all sides.

3. Remove meat and set aside.

4. Add garlic, onion, bell pepper, and zucchini in the same skillet. Sauté until softened.

5. Return the lamb to the skillet and stir together. Season with salt and pepper.

6. Cook for 5-7 minutes until the meat is cooked through.

7. Serve hot.

Nutritional Facts: (Per serving)

➤ Calories: 330

➤ Protein: 24g

➤ Carbohydrates: 8g

➤ Fat: 23g

➤ Fiber: 2g

➤ Sodium: 100mg

Indulge in the robust flavors of fried lamb paired with vibrant vegetables. An exquisite combination of protein and essential nutrients, this dish embodies the richness of gourmet home cooking.

Recipe 25: Baked Chicken Breast Stuffed

Indulge in the savory delight of baked chicken breast, skillfully stuffed for a burst of flavor with every bite. This dish is a gourmet experience and a wellspring of nutrients, perfect for health enthusiasts with discerning palates.

Servings: 4

Prepping Time: 15 minutes

Cook Time: 30 minutes

Difficulty: Intermediate

Ingredients:

- ✓ 4 boneless, skinless chicken breasts
- ✓ 1 cup spinach, chopped
- ✓ 1/2 cup feta cheese, crumbled
- ✓ 2 cloves garlic, minced
- ✓ 2 tablespoons olive oil
- ✓ Salt and pepper to taste

Step-by-Step Preparation:

1. Preheat the oven to 375°F (190°C).

2. Make a pocket in each chicken breast using a sharp knife.

3. In a bowl, combine spinach, feta cheese, and garlic.

4. Stuff each chicken breast with the spinach-feta mixture.

5. Secure with toothpicks and brush with olive oil.

6. Season with salt and pepper.

7. Place on a baking dish and bake for 30 minutes or until chicken is cooked through.

Nutritional Facts: (Per serving)

➢ Calories: 280

➢ Protein: 30g

➢ Carbohydrates: 2g

➢ Fat: 16g

➢ Fiber: 1g

➢ Sodium: 380mg

This stuffed chicken breast recipe offers the perfect blend of juiciness and health. A feast for the senses, it's bound to become a favorite in your repertoire of nutrient-rich dishes.

Recipe 26: Chicken Satay on Skewers Sprinkled with Finely

Dive into the world of flavors with Chicken Satay, a delightful skewered dish that promises a sensational experience with each bite. Marinated and grilled to perfection, then finely sprinkled, it epitomizes a nutrient-dense indulgence.

Servings: 4

Prepping Time: 20 minutes

Cook Time: 15 minutes

Difficulty: Intermediate

Ingredients:

- ✓ 500g boneless chicken breast, cut into strips
- ✓ 4 tablespoons soy sauce
- ✓ 2 tablespoons honey
- ✓ 1 teaspoon ground turmeric
- ✓ 1 teaspoon ground cumin

- ✓ 2 cloves garlic, minced
- ✓ Wooden skewers soaked in water
- ✓ Finely chopped fresh coriander for sprinkling

Step-by-Step Preparation:

1. Mix a bowl of soy sauce, honey, turmeric, cumin, and garlic.
2. Marinate chicken strips in the mixture for at least 1 hour.
3. Thread marinated chicken onto soaked skewers.
4. Grill on medium heat until fully cooked, turning occasionally.
5. Once cooked, sprinkle with finely chopped coriander.

Nutritional Facts: (Per serving)

- ➢ Calories: 220
- ➢ Protein: 30g
- ➢ Carbohydrates: 10g
- ➢ Fat: 6g
- ➢ Fiber: 0.5g
- ➢ Sodium: 820mg

Savor the rich, aromatic blend of spices and tender chicken in this Chicken Satay. An exemplary fusion of taste and nutrition, it's a dish that will leave an enduring impression on your taste buds.

Recipe 27: Caesar Roll with Chicken

Dive into the flavors of this nutrient-packed Caesar roll with chicken. The perfect blend of crispy lettuce, tender chicken, and tangy Caesar dressing wrapped in a soft roll makes this a wholesome choice for a satisfying meal.

Servings: 4

Prepping Time: 15 minutes

Cook Time: 20 minutes

Difficulty: Easy

Ingredients:

- ✓ 4 soft rolls, split horizontally
- ✓ 2 boneless, skinless chicken breasts
- ✓ 1 cup Caesar dressing
- ✓ 2 cups Romaine lettuce, chopped
- ✓ 1/4 cup Parmesan cheese, grated
- ✓ 1/2 cup croutons

✓ 1 tablespoon olive oil

✓ Salt and pepper, to taste

Step-by-Step Preparation:

1. Season chicken with salt and pepper.

2. In a skillet, heat olive oil over medium heat. Cook chicken for 7-8 minutes each side or until cooked through.

3. Slice the cooked chicken into thin strips.

4. Spread Caesar dressing on the inside of each roll.

5. Layer with lettuce, chicken strips, croutons, and sprinkle with Parmesan.

6. Close the roll and serve immediately.

Nutritional Facts: (Per serving)

➢ Calories: 450

➢ Protein: 28g

➢ Carbohydrates: 38g

➢ Dietary Fiber: 3g

➢ Sugars: 4g

➢ Fat: 20g

➢ Cholesterol: 75mg

➢ Sodium: 600mg

After a long day, indulge in this Caesar roll's refreshing taste and hearty goodness with chicken. It is nutrient-dense and tantalizes your taste buds with every bite, giving you a delightful culinary experience, you won't forget.

Recipe 28: Corn Tortilla For Cooking Tacos

Savor the authenticity of homemade corn tortillas as the foundation of your nutrient-rich chicken tacos. These tortillas bring out the essence of traditional Mexican cuisine while ensuring a healthy touch.

Servings: 8 tortillas

Prepping Time: 10 minutes

Cook Time: 20 minutes

Difficulty: Medium

Ingredients:

- ✓ 2 cups masa (corn flour)
- ✓ 1.5 cups warm water
- ✓ 1/4 teaspoon salt

Step-by-Step Preparation:

1. In a bowl, mix masa and salt.

2. Gradually add warm water, kneading continuously to form a smooth dough.

3. Divide the dough into 8 equal balls.

4. Flatten each ball between two plastic sheets using a tortilla press or rolling pin.

5. Preheat a non-stick skillet or griddle over medium-high heat.

6. Cook each tortilla on each side for 1-2 minutes until slightly puffed and golden spots appear.

7. Keep tortillas covered with a cloth to stay warm.

Nutritional Facts: (Per serving)

- Calories: 90

- Protein: 2g

- Carbohydrates: 20g

- Dietary Fiber: 2g

- Sugars: 0g

- Fat: 1g

- Cholesterol: 0mg

- Sodium: 75mg

These homemade corn tortillas take your taco nights to a whole new level. Freshly made and preservative-free, they're the perfect companion to nutrient-dense chicken fillings, offering a delightful bite every time. Dive into the true essence of Mexican fare right from your kitchen!

Recipe 29: Honey Butter Chicken Biscuit with Hot Sauce

Experience a burst of flavors with the Honey Butter Chicken Biscuit infused with a dash of hot sauce. This nutrient-dense recipe strikes a balance between sweet, buttery tenderness and spicy zest, promising a meal that's both hearty and tantalizing.

Servings: 4

Prepping Time: 20 minutes

Cook Time: 25 minutes

Difficulty: Medium

Ingredients:

- ✓ 4 boneless, skinless chicken breasts

- ✓ 4 homemade or store-bought biscuits

- ✓ 1/4 cup honey & 1/4 cup softened butter

- ✓ 1 tablespoon hot sauce (adjust to taste) & Salt and pepper, to taste

- ✓ 1 cup all-purpose flour & 1/2 cup milk

- ✓ 2 teaspoons baking powder (if making biscuits from scratch)

- ✓ 1/2 teaspoon garlic powder & Oil, for frying

Step-by-Step Preparation:

1. Season chicken with salt, pepper, and garlic powder.

2. Dredge chicken in flour, dip into milk, and then back into flour.

3. In a skillet, heat oil over medium-high and fry chicken until golden and fully cooked.

4. In a bowl, mix honey, butter, and hot sauce until smooth.

5. Split biscuits in half and generously brush the insides with the honey butter mixture.

6. Place a chicken piece inside each biscuit, drizzle more sauce if desired, and serve warm.

Nutritional Facts: (Per serving)

- ➢ Calories: 520

- ➢ Protein: 27g

- ➢ Carbohydrates: 52g

- ➢ Dietary Fiber: 1g

- ➢ Sugars: 12g

- ➢ Fat: 23g

- ➢ Cholesterol: 85mg

- ➢ Sodium: 590mg

Indulge in the irresistible combination of honey butter and spicy kick with this Chicken Biscuit. Whether it's breakfast, lunch, or dinner, this delightful dish is bound to satisfy cravings and deliver on nutrition, making every bite worth the savor.

Recipe 30: Zucchini Boat with Chicken, Beans

Embark on a culinary journey with a Zucchini boat with chicken and beans. This nutrient-dense dish combines the earthy flavors of zucchini with the heartiness of chicken and beans, crafting a wholesome and mouth-watering meal.

Servings: 4

Prepping Time: 15 minutes

Cook Time: 25 minutes

Difficulty: Medium

Ingredients:

- ✓ 4 medium zucchinis & 2 boneless, skinless chicken breasts, diced
- ✓ 1 cup cooked beans (black or pinto) & 1 onion, finely chopped
- ✓ 2 cloves garlic, minced & 1 tablespoon olive oil
- ✓ Salt and pepper, to taste & 1/2 cup shredded cheese (optional)
- ✓ 2 tablespoons fresh cilantro, chopped (for garnish)

Step-by-Step Preparation:

1. Preheat oven to 375°F (190°C).

2. Halve the zucchinis lengthwise and scoop out the flesh, leaving a 1/4-inch thick shell.

3. In a skillet, heat olive oil over medium heat. Sauté onion and garlic until translucent.

4. Add diced chicken, seasoning with salt and pepper, and cook until no longer pink.

5. Stir in beans and cook for an additional 2 minutes.

6. Stuff the zucchini halves with the chicken and bean mixture. Top with cheese if desired.

7. Place zucchini boats on a baking sheet and bake for 20 minutes or until zucchini is tender.

8. Garnish with cilantro before serving.

Nutritional Facts: (Per serving)

- Calories: 280

- Protein: 25g

- Carbohydrates: 21g

- Dietary Fiber: 6g

- Sugars: 6g & Fat: 9g

- Cholesterol: 55mg & Sodium: 240mg

Set sail on a taste adventure with these delightful Zucchini boats. Stuffed with a hearty mix of chicken and beans, they offer a symphony of flavors and nutrients in every bite. Perfect for those seeking a delectable and health-conscious dish, this recipe will surely be a hit on any table.

Chapter 04: Protein-Packed Delights

Recipe 31: Delicious Meat and Chicken Being Grilled

Discover the primal joy of the grill with this meat and chicken extravaganza. Infused with smoky undertones and marinated to perfection, every bite offers a protein-packed delight that tantalizes the senses and fuels the body.

Servings: 4

Prepping Time: 15 minutes (plus marinating time)

Cook Time: 20 minutes

Difficulty: Medium

Ingredients:

- ✓ 2 boneless chicken breasts
- ✓ 2 beef steaks (your choice of cut)
- ✓ 3 tablespoons olive oil & 2 cloves garlic, minced
- ✓ 1 tablespoon lemon juice
- ✓ 1 teaspoon dried oregano & Salt and pepper, to taste

Step-by-Step Preparation:

1. In a bowl, combine olive oil, garlic, lemon juice, oregano, salt, and pepper to form a marinade.

2. Marinate chicken and beef in the mixture for at least 2 hours, preferably overnight.

3. Preheat the grill to medium-high heat.

4. Grill chicken and beef to your preferred doneness, turning occasionally for even cooking.

5. Once done, remove from the grill and rest for a few minutes before serving.

Nutritional Facts: (Per serving)

- Calories: 350

- Protein: 35g

- Carbohydrates: 1g

- Dietary Fiber: 0g

- Sugars: 0g

- Fat: 22g

- Cholesterol: 90mg

- Sodium: 210mg

Unearth the art of grilling with this protein-rich meat and chicken recipe. Every bite promises a smoky embrace, highlighting the meat's juiciness and the marinade's richness. Whether you're a seasoned grill master or a budding chef, this dish is a testament to the timelessness of grilled delights.

Recipe 32: Mongolian Beef Stewed in Dark Soy Sauce

Delve deep into the flavors of traditional Mongolian cuisine with this sumptuous beef stew. The beef turns tender and flavorful, absorbing a delightful blend of aromatics and spices, making every bite a protein-packed delight.

Servings: 4

Prepping Time: 20 minutes

Cook Time: 2 hours

Difficulty: Medium

Ingredients:

- ✓ 1.5 pounds of beef chuck, cut into chunks
- ✓ 1/2 cup dark soy sauce & 3 cups beef broth
- ✓ 4 garlic cloves, minced & 2-inch ginger piece, thinly sliced
- ✓ 1 tablespoon brown sugar & 3 green onions, chopped
- ✓ 2 tablespoons cooking oil & 1 teaspoon toasted sesame oil

Step-by-Step Preparation:

1. In a large pot, heat the cooking oil over medium-high heat.

2. Brown the beef chunks on all sides.

3. Add garlic and ginger, sautéing until fragrant.

4. Pour in the dark soy sauce, beef broth, and brown sugar. Mix well.

5. Reduce heat to low and let the beef simmer for about 2 hours or until tender.

6. Stir in toasted sesame oil and green onions just before serving.

Nutritional Facts: (Per serving)

➤ Calories: 410

➤ Protein: 32g

➤ Carbohydrates: 8g

➤ Dietary Fiber: 1g

➤ Sugars: 4g

➤ Fat: 28g

➤ Cholesterol: 95mg

➤ Sodium: 1300mg

Take a flavorful voyage to the heart of Mongolia with this delectable beef stew. This dish promises not only a protein-packed experience but also a journey of culinary discovery. Perfect for cozy dinners or special occasions, it's a taste you won't soon forget.

Recipe 33: Still Life with Grilled Meat

Dive into an artistic culinary creation with "Still Life with grilled meat." More than just a meal, this dish becomes a canvas, where each piece of meat is perfectly grilled, showcasing the marriage of art and gastronomy, all while delivering a protein-packed punch.

Servings: 4

Prepping Time: 15 minutes

Cook Time: 20 minutes

Difficulty: Medium

Ingredients:

- ✓ 4 assorted meat cuts (like steak, chicken, and lamb)
- ✓ 3 tablespoons olive oil
- ✓ 2 cloves garlic, minced
- ✓ Salt and pepper, to taste
- ✓ Fresh herbs (like rosemary and thyme) for garnish

Step-by-Step Preparation:

1. Preheat the grill to medium-high heat.

2. Rub each meat cut with olive oil, garlic, salt, and pepper.

3. Grill each piece to the desired level of doneness, turning occasionally.

4. Once grilled, arrange the meats aesthetically on a plate or wooden board.

5. Garnish with fresh herbs and any other preferred accompaniments.

Nutritional Facts: (Per serving)

➤ Calories: 320

➤ Protein: 30g

➤ Carbohydrates: 0g

➤ Dietary Fiber: 0g

➤ Sugars: 0g

➤ Fat: 22g

➤ Cholesterol: 85mg

➤ Sodium: 580mg

"Still Life with grilled meat" transports you to a world where food transcends the plate, becoming a work of art. The tantalizing flavors and the visual appeal create a sensory delight that feeds both the soul and body— experience protein-rich gourmet dining like never before.

Recipe 34: Fried Souvlaki, Greek Salad

Embark on a Grecian gastronomic journey with "Fried Souvlaki and Greek Salad." This dish marries the succulence of perfectly fried souvlaki with the freshness of a classic Greek salad. A feast for the senses, this combination promises a protein-packed culinary delight that transports you straight to the Aegean.

Servings: 4

Prepping Time: 20 minutes

Cook Time: 15 minutes

Difficulty: Medium

Ingredients:

- ✓ 500g pork or chicken, cut into cubes & 4 tablespoons olive oil
- ✓ 2 cloves garlic, minced & 1 teaspoon oregano
- ✓ Juice of 1 lemon & Salt and pepper, to taste
- ✓ 2 tomatoes, diced & 1 cucumber, sliced
- ✓ 1 small red onion, thinly sliced
- ✓ 100g feta cheese, crumbled

✓ 50g olives (Kalamata preferred)

✓ 2 tablespoons red wine vinegar

Step-by-Step Preparation:

1. Marinate the pork or chicken cubes with half the olive oil, garlic, oregano, lemon juice, salt, and pepper. Let sit for at least 30 minutes.

2. Heat a pan over medium heat and fry the marinated meat until golden brown and fully cooked.

3. Combine tomatoes, cucumber, red onion, feta, and olives in a bowl for the salad.

4. Whisk together the remaining olive oil and red wine vinegar, then drizzle over the salad. Toss to combine.

Nutritional Facts: (Per serving)

➢ Calories: 420

➢ Protein: 30g

➢ Carbohydrates: 10g

➢ Dietary Fiber: 3g

➢ Sugars: 5g

➢ Fat: 30g

➢ Cholesterol: 85mg

➢ Sodium: 650mg

Savor the essence of Greece with the impeccable pairing of fried souvlaki and Greek salad. This dish celebrates the Mediterranean's rich flavors and offers a protein-packed treat that satiates and invigorates. Enjoy a plateful of Grecian sunshine any time of the day!

.

Recipe 35: Mediterranean Style Flatbread Pizza

Sail across the Mediterranean with every bite of this flatbread pizza. This dish offers a delightful taste experience and a generous serving of protein, perfect for those craving flavor and nourishment.

Servings: 4

Prepping Time: 15 minutes

Cook Time: 12 minutes

Difficulty: Easy

Ingredients:

- ✓ 4 flatbreads
- ✓ 1 cup mozzarella cheese, shredded
- ✓ 1/2 cup feta cheese, crumbled
- ✓ 1/4 cup sun-dried tomatoes, chopped
- ✓ 1/4 cup Kalamata olives, sliced
- ✓ 1/4 cup grilled chicken, diced

- ✓ 2 tablespoons olive oil
- ✓ 1 teaspoon oregano
- ✓ 1/4 cup fresh basil, chopped

Step-by-Step Preparation:

1. Preheat oven to 400°F (200°C).
2. Place flatbreads on a baking sheet.
3. Evenly distribute mozzarella cheese, feta cheese, sun-dried tomatoes, olives, and grilled chicken across each flatbread.
4. Drizzle with olive oil and sprinkle with oregano.
5. Bake for 10-12 minutes or until the edges are crispy and the cheese is melted.
6. Garnish with fresh basil before serving.

Nutritional Facts: (Per serving)

- ➢ Calories: 340
- ➢ Protein: 20g
- ➢ Carbohydrates: 28g
- ➢ Dietary Fiber: 3g
- ➢ Sugars: 4g
- ➢ Fat: 18g
- ➢ Cholesterol: 45mg
- ➢ Sodium: 600mg

Transport your taste buds to the Mediterranean coast with this delectable flatbread pizza. Infused with authentic flavors and brimming with protein, it's a delightful way to enjoy a quick, nourishing meal without skimping on taste. Perfect for any pizza lover looking for a healthier twist!

Recipe 36: Crunchy Beef and Quinoa Stuffed Peppers

Indulge in a harmony of textures and flavors with "Crunchy Beef and Quinoa Stuffed Peppers." This culinary masterpiece elevates the humble bell pepper with a hearty, protein-rich beef and quinoa mixture, making every bite a delightful blend of crunch and savor.

Servings: 4

Prepping Time: 20 minutes

Cook Time: 25 minutes

Difficulty: Medium

Ingredients:

- ✓ 4 large bell peppers, any color & 1/2-pound ground beef
- ✓ 1 cup cooked quinoa & 1 medium onion, diced
- ✓ 2 cloves garlic, minced & 1/2 cup tomato sauce
- ✓ 1 teaspoon ground cumin & Salt and pepper, to taste
- ✓ 1 tablespoon olive oil & 1/4 cup grated cheddar cheese (optional)

Step-by-Step Preparation:

1. Preheat oven to 375°F (190°C).

2. Cut the tops off the bell peppers and remove the seeds.

3. In a pan over medium heat, sauté onions and garlic in olive oil until translucent.

4. Add ground beef, cooking until browned.

5. Stir in quinoa, tomato sauce, cumin, salt, and pepper.

6. Spoon the beef and quinoa mixture into the bell peppers.

7. Top with cheddar cheese if using.

8. Place peppers in a baking dish and bake for 20-25 minutes until peppers are tender.

Nutritional Facts: (Per serving)

➢ Calories: 320

➢ Protein: 20g

➢ Carbohydrates: 28g

➢ Dietary Fiber: 5g

➢ Sugars: 6g

➢ Fat: 14g

➢ Cholesterol: 50mg

➢ Sodium: 420mg

Elevate your dinner table with "Crunchy Beef and Quinoa Stuffed Peppers," — a dish that promises a burst of flavors and a protein-packed punch. Whether you're catering to family or friends, this recipe guarantees satisfaction for both the palate and the appetite. Dive in and enjoy the culinary experience!

Recipe 37: Grilled BBQ Pork Belly Beef

Venture into a savory exploration with "Grilled BBQ Pork Belly Beef." This fusion of pork belly and beef captures the essence of smoky barbecue, ensuring a protein-rich feast that's not just bursting with flavors but also offers a tantalizing, charred aroma that is simply irresistible.

Servings: 4

Prepping Time: 15 minutes (plus marinating time)

Cook Time: 20 minutes

Difficulty: Medium

Ingredients:

- ✓ 1/2-pound pork belly, sliced
- ✓ 1/2-pound beef steak
- ✓ 1 cup BBQ sauce
- ✓ 2 cloves garlic, minced
- ✓ 1 tablespoon olive oil

- ✓ Salt and pepper, to taste
- ✓ 1 teaspoon smoked paprika
- ✓ 2 tablespoons apple cider vinegar

Step-by-Step Preparation:

1. Combine BBQ sauce, garlic, smoked paprika, and apple cider vinegar in a bowl.

2. Marinate pork belly and beef steak in the sauce mixture for at least 2 hours or overnight for better flavor.

3. Preheat the grill to medium-high heat and brush with olive oil.

4. Grill pork belly and beef steak until the desired doneness, basting occasionally with remaining BBQ sauce.

5. Remove from grill and let rest for a few minutes before slicing.

Nutritional Facts: (Per serving)

- ➢ Calories: 480
- ➢ Protein: 32g
- ➢ Carbohydrates: 20g
- ➢ Dietary Fiber: 0g
- ➢ Sugars: 18g
- ➢ Fat: 30g
- ➢ Cholesterol: 85mg
- ➢ Sodium: 680mg

Dive into a carnivore's dream with the "Grilled BBQ Pork Belly Beef." This dish promises a mouthful of rich, smoky flavors and a hefty dose of protein to satisfy even the most robust appetites. It's ideal for barbecues or a special dinner, a dish sure to make a lasting impression.

Recipe 38: Fried Rice with Beef - Asian Food

Satisfy your Asian cuisine cravings with this classic "Fried Rice with Beef" dish. This meal isn't just an explosion of taste but also a fantastic source of protein. Perfect for both weekday dinners and special occasions, it's a timeless favorite for a reason.

Servings: 4

Prepping Time: 15 minutes

Cook Time: 20 minutes

Difficulty: Easy

Ingredients:

- ✓ 2 cups cooked jasmine rice (preferably day-old)
- ✓ 1/2-pound beef strips
- ✓ 3 tablespoons soy sauce
- ✓ 1 onion, diced
- ✓ 2 cloves garlic, minced
- ✓ 1 cup mixed vegetables (like peas, carrots, and bell peppers)

- ✓ 2 eggs, beaten
- ✓ 2 green onions, chopped
- ✓ 1 tablespoon sesame oil
- ✓ Salt and pepper, to taste

Step-by-Step Preparation:

1. Heat a large skillet or wok over medium-high heat and add sesame oil.

2. Sauté onion and garlic until translucent.

3. Add beef strips and cook until browned.

4. Push beef to one side of the skillet and pour in beaten eggs, scrambling until fully cooked.

5. Stir in rice, mixed vegetables, and soy sauce. Cook, stirring constantly, until heated through.

6. Season with salt and pepper. Garnish with chopped green onions.

Nutritional Facts: (Per serving)

- ➤ Calories: 340
- ➤ Protein: 22g
- ➤ Carbohydrates: 40g
- ➤ Dietary Fiber: 3g
- ➤ Sugars: 2g
- ➤ Fat: 10g
- ➤ Cholesterol: 120mg
- ➤ Sodium: 800mg

Indulging in "Fried Rice with Beef" is akin to taking a delightful journey through the heart of Asian cuisine. This dish is a comforting, flavorful favorite that effortlessly brings restaurant-quality taste to your kitchen. Enjoy!

Recipe 39: Smoky Hamburger Meat Grilling

Dive into the grilling world with the "Smoky Hamburger Meat Grilling" experience. Perfectly seasoned hamburger patties kissed by smoke and flame promise an unrivaled taste and texture. It's not just a dish; it's a celebration of charred perfection and protein-rich goodness that no meat lover can resist.

Servings: 4

Prepping Time: 10 minutes

Cook Time: 15 minutes

Difficulty: Easy

Ingredients:

- ✓ 1-pound ground beef (80/20 mix)
- ✓ 1 teaspoon smoked paprika
- ✓ Salt and pepper, to taste
- ✓ 4 hamburger buns
- ✓ 1 tablespoon olive oil

✓ Optional toppings: lettuce, tomato, onions, cheese, and condiments

Step-by-Step Preparation:

1. Preheat the grill to medium-high heat.

2. Mix ground beef, smoked paprika, salt, and pepper in a bowl.

3. Divide and shape the mixture into 4 equal patties.

4. Brush the grill grates with olive oil to prevent sticking.

5. Place patties on the grill, cooking for 6-7 minutes on each side or until the desired doneness.

6. Serve on buns with optional toppings.

Nutritional Facts: (Per serving)

➢ Calories: 380

➢ Protein: 22g

➢ Carbohydrates: 23g

➢ Dietary Fiber: 1g

➢ Sugars: 3g

➢ Fat: 22g

➢ Cholesterol: 80mg

➢ Sodium: 230mg

Embrace the art of grilling with the "Smoky Hamburger Meat Grilling" dish. Each bite delivers a delicious symphony of flavors that harmoniously blend, offering a protein-packed delight. Whether for a casual cookout or a special occasion, this hamburger promises a truly unforgettable taste sensation. Enjoy!

Recipe 40: Geek Beef Souvlaki Platter with Rice

Indulge in the Mediterranean magic of the "Greek Beef Souvlaki Platter with Rice." Skewered and grilled beef chunks infused with aromatic spices complement perfectly cooked rice in this protein-packed dish. A culinary voyage to Greece, this recipe offers a feast for both the eyes and the palate.

Servings: 4

Prepping Time: 20 minutes

Cook Time: 15 minutes

Difficulty: Medium

Ingredients:

- ✓ 1-pound beef chunks or steak, cubed
- ✓ 1 tablespoon olive oil
- ✓ 2 cloves garlic, minced
- ✓ 1 teaspoon dried oregano
- ✓ Juice of 1 lemon

✓ Salt and pepper, to taste

✓ 2 cups cooked long-grain rice

✓ Wooden skewers soaked in water

Step-by-Step Preparation:

1. Combine olive oil, minced garlic, oregano, lemon juice, salt, and pepper in a bowl.

2. Add beef chunks, ensuring they're well-coated, and marinate for at least 1 hour.

3. Preheat the grill to medium-high heat.

4. Thread the beef onto the soaked skewers.

5. Grill for 6-7 minutes on each side or until desired doneness.

6. Serve the beef souvlaki over a bed of rice.

Nutritional Facts: (Per serving)

➢ Calories: 390

➢ Protein: 28g

➢ Carbohydrates: 40g

➢ Dietary Fiber: 1g

➢ Sugars: 1g

➢ Fat: 12g

➢ Cholesterol: 70mg

➢ Sodium: 90mg

The "Greek Beef Souvlaki Platter with Rice" is more than just a dish; it's an experience. Embark on a gastronomic journey to the heart of Greece, savoring every bite of this protein-rich delight. Ideal for gatherings or family dinners, this dish effortlessly brings the Mediterranean's vibrant flavors to your dining table. Bon appétit!

Chapter 05: Plant-based Protein Rich Recipes

Recipe 41: Spicy Chickpea and Spinach Stew

Dive into a hearty warm bowl with the "Spicy Chickpea and Spinach Stew." Brimming with flavors and loaded with plant-based proteins, this stew is not only nourishing but also tantalizingly delicious. Whether you're a vegan, vegetarian, or just a lover of great food, this recipe is set to become a cherished favorite.

Servings: 4

Prepping Time: 15 minutes

Cook Time: 30 minutes

Difficulty: Easy

Ingredients:

- ✓ 2 cups cooked chickpeas (or canned, drained)
- ✓ 4 cups fresh spinach, roughly chopped & 1 onion, diced

- ✓ 2 cloves garlic, minced & 1 can (14 oz) diced tomatoes

- ✓ 2 cups vegetable broth & 1 teaspoon smoked paprika

- ✓ 1/2 teaspoon cayenne pepper & 2 tablespoons olive oil

- ✓ Salt and pepper, to taste

Step-by-Step Preparation:

1. In a large pot, heat olive oil over medium heat.

2. Sauté onion and garlic until translucent.

3. Add smoked paprika, cayenne pepper, and season with salt and pepper.

4. Stir in chickpeas, diced tomatoes, and vegetable broth.

5. Bring to a boil, then reduce to a simmer for 20 minutes.

6. Stir in chopped spinach, cooking until wilted.

7. Adjust seasoning if needed, and serve hot.

Nutritional Facts: (Per serving)

- ➢ Calories: 220

- ➢ Protein: 9g

- ➢ Carbohydrates: 35g

- ➢ Dietary Fiber: 8g

- ➢ Sugars: 6g

- ➢ Fat: 7g & Cholesterol: 0mg & Sodium: 500mg

The "Spicy Chickpea and Spinach Stew" is an ode to plant-based, protein-rich dishes. It seamlessly combines health with indulgence, ensuring that every spoonful is a delightful burst of flavor. Whether served as a cozy dinner or a nourishing lunch, this stew promises both satisfaction and wellness in a bowl. Enjoy!

Recipe 42: Deep Fried Crispy Tofu in Small Bite

Delve into the crunchy delight of "Deep Fried Crispy Tofu in Small Bites." Perfectly golden and crispy on the outside, yet soft and tender within, these tofu bites are the epitome of plant-based indulgence. Ideal as appetizers or snacking treats, they bring a protein-packed punch to your plate.

Servings: 4

Prepping Time: 15 minutes

Cook Time: 10 minutes

Difficulty: Easy

Ingredients:

- ✓ 14 oz block firm tofu, pressed and cubed
- ✓ 1/2 cup cornstarch
- ✓ Salt and pepper, to taste
- ✓ 1 teaspoon garlic powder (optional)
- ✓ Oil for frying & Soy sauce or dip of choice for serving

Step-by-Step Preparation:

1. After pressing the tofu, cut it into small bite-sized cubes.

2. Mix cornstarch, salt, pepper, and garlic powder in a bowl.

3. Gently coat tofu cubes in the cornstarch mixture.

4. Heat oil in a frying pan over medium-high heat.

5. Carefully place tofu cubes into the hot oil and fry until golden brown on all sides.

6. Remove and drain on paper towels.

7. Serve hot with soy sauce or preferred dip.

Nutritional Facts: (Per serving)

➢ Calories: 210

➢ Protein: 12g

➢ Carbohydrates: 14g

➢ Dietary Fiber: 1g

➢ Sugars: 0g

➢ Fat: 12g

➢ Cholesterol: 0mg

➢ Sodium: 20mg

Embrace the allure of "Deep Fried Crispy Tofu in Small Bites" and elevate your snack game. Every bite celebrates texture and taste, offering a protein-rich, plant-based treat that vegans and non-vegans will adore. Dip, munch, and relish the crispy goodness!

Recipe 43: Vegan Lentil Burger with Arugula

Indulge in the flavorful depths of the "Vegan Lentil Burger with Arugula." These burgers don't just bring the plant-based protein power of lentils; they couple it with the peppery kick of arugula for an utterly satisfying vegan delight. Dive into this wholesome treat and experience veganism at its finest.

Servings: 4

Prepping Time: 20 minutes

Cook Time: 15 minutes

Difficulty: Medium

Ingredients:

- ✓ 2 cups cooked green lentils & 1/2 cup breadcrumbs
- ✓ 1/4 cup finely chopped onion & 2 garlic cloves, minced
- ✓ 2 tablespoons ground flaxseed (as a binder)
- ✓ 1 tablespoon soy sauce & 1 teaspoon smoked paprika
- ✓ Salt and pepper, to taste & 1 cup fresh arugula
- ✓ 4 vegan burger buns & Vegan mayo or dressing of choice

Step-by-Step Preparation:

1. In a food processor, blend lentils until semi-smooth.

2. Transfer to a bowl and mix with breadcrumbs, onion, garlic, flaxseed, soy sauce, smoked paprika, salt, and pepper.

3. Form the mixture into four patties.

4. Over medium heat, cook the patties in a skillet for 7-8 minutes on each side or until golden.

5. To serve, place a cake on each bun, top with arugula and vegan mayo or dressing.

Nutritional Facts: (Per serving)

➢ Calories: 320

➢ Protein: 18g

➢ Carbohydrates: 54g

➢ Dietary Fiber: 10g

➢ Sugars: 6g

➢ Fat: 5g

➢ Cholesterol: 0mg

➢ Sodium: 390mg

A rendezvous with the "Vegan Lentil Burger with Arugula" promises a burst of flavors with every bite. This burger is a testament to the fact that healthy can be tasty too. It's a recipe worth relishing, perfect for BBQs, picnics, or a cozy dinner.

Recipe 44: Warm Quinoa and Pumpkin Salad

Dive into a bowlful of vibrant flavors and textures with the "Warm Quinoa and Pumpkin Salad." This salad epitomizes nutritious elegance. It's not just a visual delight; it's a symphony of health, brimming with plant-based protein goodness.

Servings: 4

Prepping Time: 20 minutes

Cook Time: 25 minutes

Difficulty: Easy

Ingredients:

- ✓ 1 cup quinoa (rinsed and drained)
- ✓ 2 cups diced pumpkin
- ✓ 2 tablespoons olive oil
- ✓ 1/4 cup roasted pumpkin seeds
- ✓ 1/4 cup chopped fresh parsley

- ✓ 2 green onions, sliced
- ✓ Juice of 1 lemon
- ✓ Salt and pepper, to taste

Step-by-Step Preparation:

1. In a saucepan, cook quinoa according to package instructions. Fluff with a fork and set aside.

2. In a separate pan, sauté pumpkin dice in olive oil until tender and slightly caramelized.

3. Combine warm quinoa, sautéed pumpkin, pumpkin seeds, parsley, and green onions in a large mixing bowl.

4. Drizzle with lemon juice, then season with salt and pepper. Toss to combine.

Nutritional Facts: (Per serving)

- ➢ Calories: 260
- ➢ Protein: 8g
- ➢ Carbohydrates: 45g
- ➢ Dietary Fiber: 6g
- ➢ Sugars: 3g
- ➢ Fat: 8g
- ➢ Cholesterol: 0mg
- ➢ Sodium: 15mg

The "Warm Quinoa and Pumpkin Salad" is your passport to a nourishing culinary adventure. With every forkful, experience a mélange of flavors and textures, all while fueling your body with plant-based protein. Perfect as a standalone dish or a side, it's a staple for those who cherish health without compromising taste.

Recipe 45: Roasted Vegan Lentil Meatballs

Indulge in the savory richness of roasted vegan lentil meatballs, a delightful fusion of hearty flavors and plant-based nutrition. Perfect for those seeking a protein-packed alternative without compromising on taste.

Servings: 4

Prepping Time: 20 minutes

Cook Time: 30 minutes

Difficulty: Moderate

Ingredients:

- ✓ 1 cup cooked green lentils
- ✓ 1/2 cup breadcrumbs
- ✓ 1/4 cup finely chopped onions
- ✓ 2 cloves garlic, minced
- ✓ 2 tbsp olive oil
- ✓ 1 tsp dried oregano
- ✓ Salt and pepper to taste

- ✓ 1 tbsp fresh parsley, chopped
- ✓ 1/2 cup vegetable broth

Step-by-Step Preparation:

1. Preheat oven to 375°F (190°C).

2. Combine lentils, onions, garlic, breadcrumbs, oregano, salt, and pepper in a food processor. Pulse until well mixed.

3. Place the mixture into small balls on a baking sheet lined with parchment paper.

4. Drizzle with olive oil.

5. Bake for 25-30 minutes or until the meatballs turn golden brown.

6. Heat the vegetable broth in a pan in the last 10 minutes of baking and simmer the meatballs for added moisture and flavor.

7. Garnish with fresh parsley before serving.

Nutritional Facts: (Per serving)

- ➤ Calories: 220 kcal
- ➤ Protein: 12g
- ➤ Carbohydrates: 30g
- ➤ Dietary Fiber: 10g
- ➤ Sugars: 2g
- ➤ Fat: 6g
- ➤ Sodium: 200mg

Bite into the robust flavors of these lentil meatballs and relish the goodness of nature's bounties. It's more than just a meal; it's a testament that vegan dishes can be delectable, nourishing, and satisfying all at once. Enjoy this culinary masterpiece alongside your favorite pasta or salad.

Recipe 46: Colorful Mexican Quinoa Stuffed

Discover the vibrant flavors of Mexico in every bite with this Colorful Mexican Quinoa Stuffed dish. A nutritious medley of quinoa, beans, and veggies, it's an exotic treat that promises taste and health in every forkful.

Servings: 4

Prepping Time: 20 minutes

Cook Time: 25 minutes

Difficulty: Moderate

Ingredients:

- ✓ 1 cup cooked quinoa & 1/2 cup black beans, rinsed and drained
- ✓ 1/2 cup corn kernels & 1 red bell pepper, diced
- ✓ 1 avocado, diced & 2 green onions, finely chopped
- ✓ 1/4 cup fresh cilantro, chopped & 1 lime, juiced
- ✓ 2 tbsp olive oil & Salt and pepper to taste
- ✓ 4 large bell peppers (for stuffing)

Step-by-Step Preparation:

1. Preheat oven to 375°F (190°C).

2. Combine quinoa, black beans, corn, diced red bell pepper, avocado, green onions, cilantro, lime juice, olive oil, salt, and pepper in a large mixing bowl. Mix well.

3. Slice the tops of the 4 large bell peppers and remove the seeds.

4. Stuff each bell pepper with the quinoa mixture, pressing gently.

5. Place the stuffed bell peppers in a baking dish.

6. Cover with foil and bake for 20-25 minutes until peppers are tender.

7. Serve hot, garnished with extra cilantro if desired.

Nutritional Facts: (Per serving)

➢ Calories: 280 kcal

➢ Protein: 8g

➢ Carbohydrates: 42g

➢ Dietary Fiber: 8g

➢ Sugars: 6g

➢ Fat: 10g

➢ Sodium: 80mg

Dive into a symphony of textures and tastes with these Colorful Mexican Quinoa Stuffed bell peppers. It's a hearty meal that delights the senses while fueling the body with plant-based protein. Whether it's a weekday dinner or a festive gathering, this dish will surely steal the spotlight.

Recipe 47: Sushi Hot Roll with Salmon

Experience a culinary fusion with the Sushi Hot Roll with Salmon, where traditional sushi meets modern flair. While salmon usually isn't plant-based, this rendition uses innovative ingredients to capture the essence of sushi, delivering both flavor and plant-powered protein.

Servings: 4

Prepping Time: 30 minutes

Cook Time: 10 minutes

Difficulty: Advanced

Ingredients:

- ✓ 2 cups sushi rice, cooked and cooled

- ✓ 2 tbsp rice vinegar

- ✓ 1 cup vegan salmon substitute (e.g., tomato or carrot-based)

- ✓ 1/2 cup tempura batter & 2 nori sheets & 1 avocado, sliced

- ✓ Soy sauce for dipping & Wasabi and pickled ginger for serving

Step-by-Step Preparation:

1. Mix the rice vinegar into the sushi rice until well combined.

2. Place a nori sheet on a bamboo sushi mat, shiny side down.

3. Spread an even layer of sushi rice onto the nori, leaving a 1-inch border at the top.

4. Lay vegan salmon substitute and avocado slices in a line down the center.

5. Roll tightly using the bamboo mat.

6. Dip the sushi roll into the tempura batter, ensuring it's fully coated.

7. Fry in hot oil until golden brown.

8. Slice into bite-sized pieces and serve with soy sauce, wasabi, and pickled ginger.

Nutritional Facts: (Per serving)

➤ Calories: 320 kcal

➤ Protein: 6g

➤ Carbohydrates: 60g

➤ Dietary Fiber: 4g

➤ Sugars: 3g

➤ Fat: 7g

➤ Sodium: 300mg

Embark on a delightful gastronomic journey with the Sushi Hot Roll with Salmon, a re-imagination of classic sushi. This dish retains the iconic flavors of sushi while packing a protein punch. Perfect for sushi lovers looking for an innovative twist on their favorite meal.

Recipe 48: Salmon Sautéed in Organic Butter

Dive into the elegance of the sea with a dish that promises unparalleled taste and nutrition. The Salmon Sautéed in Organic Butter offers a mouth-watering juxtaposition of tender salmon and rich butter, with a plant-based twist sure to impress.

Servings: 4

Prepping Time: 10 minutes

Cook Time: 10 minutes

Difficulty: Easy

Ingredients:

- ✓ 4 salmon fillets

- ✓ 3 tbsp organic plant-based butter (e.g., almond or cashew-based butter)

- ✓ 2 garlic cloves, minced

- ✓ 1 lemon, juiced

- ✓ Salt and pepper to taste

✓ Fresh parsley, finely chopped for garnish

Step-by-Step Preparation:

1. Heat plant-based butter in a skillet over medium heat.

2. Once melted, add minced garlic and sauté until fragrant.

3. Season salmon fillets with salt and pepper.

4. Place the salmon in the skillet, skin side down.

5. Cook 4-5 minutes on each side until the salmon is golden and flakes easily.

6. Drizzle lemon juice over the salmon during the last minute of cooking.

7. Garnish with fresh parsley before serving.

Nutritional Facts: (Per serving)

➢ Calories: 320 kcal

➢ Protein: 34g

➢ Carbohydrates: 1g

➢ Dietary Fiber: 0g

➢ Sugars: 0g

➢ Fat: 20g

➢ Sodium: 80mg

Celebrate the simplicity and sophistication of Salmon Sautéed in Organic Butter. This dish seamlessly marries the classic flavors of the ocean with the benefits of plant-based ingredients, delivering both a protein punch and an epicurean delight. It's dining at its finest, ensuring every bite is nutritious and delectably memorable.

Recipe 49: Medium-roasted Coffee Beans are Smoky

Awaken your senses with the rich aroma and smoky undertones of Medium-Roasted Coffee Beans. This blend celebrates the coffee bean's journey, capturing its essence in the perfect medium roast, promising caffeine-kick and sumptuous flavor.

Servings: Makes about 4 cups of brewed coffee

Prepping Time: 5 minutes

Cook Time: No cook time (Brew time varies by method)

Difficulty: Easy

Ingredients:

- ✓ 4 tablespoons medium-roasted coffee beans, coarsely ground

- ✓ 4 cups of filtered water

- ✓ Optional: sugar or plant-based milk to taste

Step-by-Step Preparation:

1. Start with fresh, filtered water, heated to just below boiling (about 200°F or 93°C).

2. Place the coarsely ground coffee beans in your preferred coffee maker or French press.

3. Pour the hot water over the coffee grounds.

4. Brew according to your coffee maker's instructions or, if using a French press, let steep for 4 minutes.

5. Press the plunger down slowly, and pour into your favorite mug.

6. Add sugar or plant-based milk to taste, if desired.

Nutritional Facts: (Per serving)

➤ Calories: 2 kcal

➤ Protein: 0.3g

➤ Carbohydrates: 0g

➤ Dietary Fiber: 0g

➤ Sugars: 0g

➤ Fat: 0g

➤ Sodium: 5mg

Embrace the allure of Medium-Roasted Coffee Beans, where every sip is a symphony of smoky flavors. Whether it's a morning ritual or an afternoon pick-me-up, this coffee ensures that the unparalleled joy of a well-brewed cup accompanies every moment. Enjoy the journey, one brew at a time.

Recipe 50: Asian Inspired Edamame Salad

Embark on a culinary journey to the East with the Asian Inspired Edamame Salad. This dish blends the vibrant flavors of Asia with the nutritious punch of edamame, creating a salad that's as delightful to the palate as it is beneficial for the body.

Servings: 4

Prepping Time: 15 minutes

Cook Time: 10 minutes

Difficulty: Easy

Ingredients:

- ✓ 2 cups shelled edamame, cooked
- ✓ 1 red bell pepper, thinly sliced
- ✓ 2 carrots, julienned & 4 green onions, chopped
- ✓ 1/4 cup fresh cilantro, chopped & 3 tbsp soy sauce or tamari
- ✓ 1 tbsp sesame oil

- ✓ 1 tbsp rice vinegar
- ✓ 1 tsp fresh ginger, grated
- ✓ 1 tbsp sesame seeds
- ✓ Optional: chili flakes to taste

Step-by-Step Preparation:

1. Combine edamame, red bell pepper, carrots, and green onions in a large mixing bowl.

2. Whisk together soy sauce or tamari, sesame oil, rice vinegar, and grated ginger in a separate small bowl.

3. Pour the dressing over the edamame mixture and toss to coat evenly.

4. Garnish with cilantro, sesame seeds, and chili flakes if using.

5. Chill for at least 30 minutes before serving to allow flavors to meld.

Nutritional Facts: (Per serving)

- ➢ Calories: 210 kcal
- ➢ Protein: 13g
- ➢ Carbohydrates: 20g
- ➢ Dietary Fiber: 8g
- ➢ Sugars: 5g
- ➢ Fat: 9g
- ➢ Sodium: 800mg

Relish the fusion of crisp vegetables and tantalizing Asian flavors in the Asian Inspired Edamame Salad. This refreshing dish promises taste and nourishment, making it a perfect choice for a light lunch or a flavorful side. Let every bite transport you to the heart of Asia while enjoying the benefits of plant-based protein.

Chapter 06: Breakfast Delights

Recipe 51: Little Banana Split and Some Ice-Cream

Indulge in a morning treat that's whimsical and delightful with the Little Banana Split and Some Ice-Cream. This breakfast rendition of a classic dessert offers a playful start to your day, combining the sweetness of bananas with the creaminess of ice cream.

Servings: 2

Prepping Time: 10 minutes

Cook Time: 0 minutes

Difficulty: Easy

Ingredients:

- ✓ 2 ripe bananas, peeled and halved

- ✓ 4 scoops of your favorite ice cream (can use dairy-free)

- ✓ 2 tbsp chocolate syrup
- ✓ 1 tbsp chopped nuts (e.g., almonds, walnuts)
- ✓ Fresh berries for garnish & Whipped cream (optional)
- ✓ A sprinkle of granola for crunch (optional)

Step-by-Step Preparation:

1. Lay out two serving dishes.
2. Place two banana halves on each plate, forming a "V" shape.
3. Scoop two scoops of ice cream into the center of each banana pair.
4. Drizzle with chocolate syrup.
5. Garnish with chopped nuts and fresh berries.
6. If desired, top with whipped cream and a sprinkle of granola.

Nutritional Facts: (Per serving)

- ➤ Calories: 320 kcal
- ➤ Protein: 5g
- ➤ Carbohydrates: 52g
- ➤ Dietary Fiber: 4g
- ➤ Sugars: 37g
- ➤ Fat: 12g
- ➤ Sodium: 75mg

Elevate your breakfast experience with the Little Banana Split and Some Ice-Cream. This dish isn't just a treat for the taste buds; it's a celebration of morning joy. Whether it's a special weekend breakfast or a cheerful weekday surprise, this dish promises a delightful burst of flavor and happiness with every bite.

Recipe 52: Waffles with Peanut Butter

Wake up to the comforting embrace of Waffles with Peanut Butter, a breakfast dish that combines the crispy charm of waffles with the creamy richness of peanut butter. It's a symphony of textures and flavors, perfect for mornings that deserve a special touch.

Servings: 4

Prepping Time: 10 minutes

Cook Time: 15 minutes

Difficulty: Easy

Ingredients:

- ✓ 2 cups waffle mix
- ✓ 1 1/2 cups water or milk
- ✓ 1/4 cup melted butter or oil
- ✓ 1/2 cup creamy peanut butter (or to taste)
- ✓ Maple syrup (optional) & Fresh fruits for garnish (like strawberries or bananas)

Step-by-Step Preparation:

1. Preheat your waffle iron according to its manufacturer's instructions.

2. Combine waffle mix, water or milk, and melted butter or oil in a mixing bowl. Stir until smooth.

3. Pour the batter onto the heated waffle iron and cook according to the device's guidelines.

4. Once the waffles are ready, spread a generous amount of peanut butter over each waffle.

5. Drizzle with maple syrup if desired, and garnish with fresh fruits.

Nutritional Facts: (Per serving)

➢ Calories: 450 kcal

➢ Protein: 12g

➢ Carbohydrates: 50g

➢ Dietary Fiber: 3g

➢ Sugars: 12g

➢ Fat: 25g

➢ Sodium: 350mg

Embark on a culinary adventure as you bite into the delectable Waffles with Peanut Butter. It's not just a breakfast dish; it's an experience that warms the heart and kickstarts your day. Let this breakfast delight be your go-to choose for those mornings when ordinary won't do.

Recipe 53: Hand Holding a Burrito with a Bite

Dive into the flavorsome world of breakfast burritos with the enticing "Hand Holding a Burrito with a Bite." Crafted with care, this dish melds morning favorites into a portable delight, ensuring that each bite is filled with layers of breakfast joy.

Servings: 4

Prepping Time: 15 minutes

Cook Time: 10 minutes

Difficulty: Easy

Ingredients:

- ✓ 4 large tortillas
- ✓ 6 eggs, whisked
- ✓ 1 cup shredded cheese (cheddar or Monterey Jack)
- ✓ 1/2 cup salsa
- ✓ 1/2 cup cooked and crumbled breakfast sausage or bacon
- ✓ 1/2 cup diced bell peppers

- ✓ 1/4 cup chopped onions
- ✓ Salt and pepper to taste
- ✓ 2 tbsp cooking oil or butter

Step-by-Step Preparation:

1. In a large skillet, heat oil or butter over medium heat.
2. Add onions and bell peppers, sautéing until softened.
3. Pour in the whisked eggs, stirring continuously until nearly set.
4. Mix in the crumbled breakfast sausage or bacon.
5. Warm tortillas as per package instructions.
6. Lay out each tortilla, spreading a layer of cheese, the egg mixture, and a spoonful of salsa.
7. Roll up the tortilla, fold in the sides, and serve immediately.

Nutritional Facts: (Per serving)

- ➤ Calories: 490 kcal
- ➤ Protein: 23g
- ➤ Carbohydrates: 30g
- ➤ Dietary Fiber: 2g
- ➤ Sugars: 3g
- ➤ Fat: 30g
- ➤ Sodium: 900mg

Starting the day with a "Hand Holding a Burrito with a Bite" is choosing a symphony of textures and flavors conveniently wrapped in one hand-held package. Whether it's an on-the-go morning or a leisurely weekend, this breakfast burrito will surely be a favorite, offering nourishment and sheer culinary delight.

Recipe 54: Gluten-free Pancakes with Berries

Discover the magic of morning delights with "Gluten-free Pancakes with Berries." Soft, fluffy, and flavorful, these pancakes promise a wholesome start to the day, adorned with nature's sweet gems and tailored for those seeking gluten-free alternatives.

Servings: 4

Prepping Time: 10 minutes

Cook Time: 15 minutes

Difficulty: Easy

Ingredients:

- ✓ 1 cup gluten-free all-purpose flour
- ✓ 1 tbsp sugar (or sweetener of choice)
- ✓ 1 tsp baking powder & 1/4 tsp salt
- ✓ 1 cup almond milk (or milk of choice)
- ✓ 1 large egg & 2 tbsp melted coconut oil or butter
- ✓ 1 tsp vanilla extract
- ✓ 1 cup mixed fresh berries (e.g., blueberries, raspberries, strawberries)

Step-by-Step Preparation:

1. Whisk together the flour, sugar, baking powder, and salt in a large bowl.

2. Combine milk, egg, melted coconut oil or butter, and vanilla extract in another bowl.

3. Pour the wet ingredients into the dry, stirring until just combined.

4. Heat a non-stick skillet over medium heat. For each pancake, pour 1/4 cup of batter onto the skillet.

5. Add a sprinkle of berries to each pancake.

6. Cook until bubbles appear on the surface, then flip and cook until browned.

Nutritional Facts: (Per serving)

➢ Calories: 210 kcal

➢ Protein: 5g

➢ Carbohydrates: 30g

➢ Dietary Fiber: 4g

➢ Sugars: 10g

➢ Fat: 8g

➢ Sodium: 250mg

Indulge in the simple pleasure of "Gluten-free Pancakes with Berries" and kickstart your mornings with a dance of flavors. These pancakes, tender and naturally sweetened by berries, not only satiate the taste buds but also offer a gluten-free haven for breakfast enthusiasts. Enjoy a plateful of health and happiness!

Recipe 55: Spinach and Feta Frittata in a Skillet

Dive into a Mediterranean-inspired morning with the "Spinach and Feta Frittata in a Skillet." This savory delight marries the earthy goodness of spinach with the tangy richness of feta, all bound together in a fluffy egg canvas, ensuring a hearty start to the day.

Servings: 4

Prepping Time: 10 minutes

Cook Time: 20 minutes

Difficulty: Easy

Ingredients:

- ✓ 8 large eggs
- ✓ 1 cup fresh spinach, roughly chopped
- ✓ 1/2 cup crumbled feta cheese
- ✓ 1/4 cup diced onions
- ✓ 1/4 cup diced bell peppers
- ✓ 2 tbsp olive oil or butter

✓ Salt and pepper to taste

✓ Fresh herbs (e.g., dill, parsley) for garnish

Step-by-Step Preparation:

1. In a bowl, whisk together the eggs, salt, and pepper.

2. In a skillet, heat olive oil or butter over medium heat.

3. Sauté onions and bell peppers until translucent.

4. Add in the spinach, cooking until just wilted.

5. Pour the egg mixture over the vegetables and sprinkle the feta cheese.

6. Cook on medium-low heat until the edges are set.

7. Place the skillet under a broiler for 2-3 minutes until the top is golden and set.

8. Garnish with fresh herbs and serve.

Nutritional Facts: (Per serving)

➤ Calories: 260 kcal

➤ Protein: 16g

➤ Carbohydrates: 4g

➤ Dietary Fiber: 1g

➤ Sugars: 2g

➤ Fat: 20g

➤ Sodium: 410mg

Elevate your breakfast repertoire with the "Spinach and Feta Frittata in a Skillet." This dish doesn't just nourish the body; it delights the palate, bringing the vibrant flavors of the Mediterranean straight to your breakfast table. Let every forkful be an ode to fresh, wholesome ingredients and culinary craftsmanship.

Recipe 56: Peanut Butter and Dark Chocolate

Start your day with a delectable fusion of "Peanut Butter and Dark Chocolate." This tantalizing duo elevates morning rituals, melding creamy peanut butter's richness with the bitter-sweet allure of dark chocolate, making every bite an opulent indulgence.

Servings: 2

Prepping Time: 5 minutes

Cook Time: 0 minutes

Difficulty: Easy

Ingredients:

- ✓ 4 tbsp creamy peanut butter
- ✓ 50g dark chocolate, roughly chopped
- ✓ 2 slices of whole grain bread (or bread of choice)
- ✓ A pinch of sea salt (optional)
- ✓ Fresh berries for garnish (optional)

Step-by-Step Preparation:

1. Toast the bread slices to your preferred level of crispiness.

2. Spread an even layer of peanut butter over each toasted piece.

3. Sprinkle the chopped dark chocolate over the peanut butter.

4. If desired, sprinkle a pinch of sea salt on top.

5. Garnish with fresh berries if using, and serve immediately.

Nutritional Facts: (Per serving)

➤ Calories: 320 kcal

➤ Protein: 10g

➤ Carbohydrates: 28g

➤ Dietary Fiber: 4g

➤ Sugars: 12g

➤ Fat: 20g

➤ Sodium: 200mg

Let "Peanut Butter and Dark Chocolate" be the zenith of your breakfast cravings. Enjoy this gastronomic affair with every bite!

Recipe 57: Healthy Blueberry and Raspberry

Embrace the morning with the vibrant duo of "Healthy Blueberry and Raspberry." This refreshing dish celebrates the juicy goodness of blueberries and raspberries, bringing a burst of antioxidants and natural sweetness to energize your day most delightfully.

Servings: 2

Prepping Time: 5 minutes

Cook Time: 0 minutes

Difficulty: Easy

Ingredients:

- ✓ 1 cup fresh blueberries
- ✓ 1 cup fresh raspberries
- ✓ 2 tbsp honey or maple syrup (optional)
- ✓ A sprinkle of chia seeds (optional)
- ✓ Fresh mint leaves for garnish

Step-by-Step Preparation:

1. In a mixing bowl, gently combine blueberries and raspberries.

2. If desired, drizzle honey or maple syrup over the berries for added sweetness.

3. Toss the berries gently to combine.

4. Serve in individual bowls, sprinkled with chia seeds if using.

5. Garnish with fresh mint leaves.

Nutritional Facts: (Per serving)

➢ Calories: 90 kcal

➢ Protein: 1g

➢ Carbohydrates: 22g

➢ Dietary Fiber: 5g

➢ Sugars: 15g

➢ Fat: 0.5g

➢ Sodium: 1mg

Kickstart your day with the natural zest of "Healthy Blueberry and Raspberry." As a symphony of flavors and nutrients, this dish nourishes the body and elevates the mood. Perfect for those looking for a light, wholesome, and tantalizingly tangy start to their morning.

Recipe 58: Tofu Scramble Toast with Green Onion

Elevate your mornings with the "Tofu Scramble Toast with Green Onion," a delightful fusion of creamy tofu and the piquant freshness of green onions. This plant-based masterpiece provides both a protein boost and a zesty flavor kick, ensuring a nourishing and memorable breakfast.

Servings: 2

Prepping Time: 10 minutes

Cook Time: 15 minutes

Difficulty: Easy

Ingredients:

- ✓ 200g firm tofu, crumbled
- ✓ 2 green onions, finely chopped
- ✓ 1 tbsp olive oil
- ✓ 1/4 tsp turmeric powder (for color)

✓ Salt and pepper to taste

✓ 2 slices of whole-grain toast

✓ Fresh herbs (e.g., parsley) for garnish (optional)

Step-by-Step Preparation:

1. Heat olive oil in a skillet over medium heat.

2. Add the crumbled tofu to the skillet.

3. Sprinkle in the turmeric, salt, and pepper. Stir well.

4. Cook the tofu until it's lightly golden and resembles scrambled eggs.

5. Stir in the chopped green onions and cook for an additional 2 minutes.

6. Toast the bread slices.

7. Generously top each toast slice with the tofu scramble.

8. Garnish with fresh herbs if desired, and serve hot.

Nutritional Facts: (Per serving)

➤ Calories: 210 kcal

➤ Protein: 12g

➤ Carbohydrates: 20g

➤ Dietary Fiber: 3g

➤ Sugars: 2g

➤ Fat: 10g

➤ Sodium: 150mg

Savor the charm of "Tofu Scramble Toast with Green Onion" as it transforms an ordinary morning into an extraordinary culinary experience. This dish combines health and flavor in perfect harmony, setting the tone for a productive and delightful day ahead. Relish every bite of this breakfast gem!

Recipe 59: Chocolate and Cocoa Mixed with Milk

Begin your morning with a luscious blend of "Chocolate and Cocoa Mixed with Milk." This silky, rich beverage is a timeless classic, embracing the deep flavors of chocolate and cocoa, complemented by the creamy texture of milk. It's more than just a drink; it's a moment of indulgence to kickstart your day.

Servings: 2

Prepping Time: 5 minutes

Cook Time: 5 minutes

Difficulty: Easy

Ingredients:

- ✓ 2 cups milk (whole or any alternative)
- ✓ 2 tbsp cocoa powder, unsweetened
- ✓ 50g dark chocolate, roughly chopped
- ✓ 2 tbsp sugar or sweetener of choice (optional)
- ✓ A pinch of salt & Whipped cream for garnish (optional)

Step-by-Step Preparation:

1. Heat the milk over medium heat in a saucepan until it's warm but not boiling.

2. Add the cocoa powder, dark chocolate, sugar (if using), and a pinch of salt.

3. Whisk until the chocolate is completely melted and the mixture is smooth.

4. Once heated to your desired temperature, remove from heat.

5. Pour into mugs and top with whipped cream if desired.

Nutritional Facts: (Per serving)

➤ Calories: 250 kcal

➤ Protein: 8g

➤ Carbohydrates: 30g

➤ Dietary Fiber: 2g

➤ Sugars: 25g

➤ Fat: 12g

➤ Sodium: 100mg

Dive into the comforting embrace of "Chocolate and Cocoa Mixed with Milk" and let it warm your soul. This beverage promises a journey of flavors, from the deep, earthy tons of cocoa to the luxurious sweetness of chocolate. Perfect for those mornings when you need a dose of delight with your dawn.

Recipe 60: Kiwi yogurt Smoothies' Juice

Experience a rejuvenating start to your day with the "Kiwi Yogurt Smoothies' Juice." This velvety concoction, brimming with the tangy flavor of kiwi and the smooth richness of yogurt, offers an irresistible treat that's both refreshing and nutritious.

Servings: 2

Prepping Time: 10 minutes

Cook Time: 0 minutes (Blend time: 2 minutes)

Difficulty: Easy

Ingredients:

- ✓ 2 ripe kiwis, peeled and sliced

- ✓ 1 cup plain yogurt (or Greek yogurt for a thicker consistency)

- ✓ 1 tbsp honey or maple syrup (optional)

- ✓ 1/2 cup ice cubes & A splash of milk or water for desired consistency

- ✓ Fresh kiwi slices for garnish

Step-by-Step Preparation:

1. Combine kiwis, yogurt, honey (if using), and ice cubes in a blender.

2. Blend on high until smooth.

3. Adjust consistency with a splash of milk or water if needed.

4. Pour into glasses and garnish with fresh kiwi slices.

Nutritional Facts: (Per serving)

➢ Calories: 120 kcal

➢ Protein: 5g

➢ Carbohydrates: 25g

➢ Dietary Fiber: 3g

➢ Sugars: 18g

➢ Fat: 2g

➢ Sodium: 50mg

The "Kiwi Yogurt Smoothies' Juice" epitomizes morning delight. Every sip is a reminder of nature's bountiful goodness. It's not just a smoothie; it's a refreshing dance of flavors, perfect to invigorate your senses and set the tone for the day. Enjoy!

Chapter 07: Low-Carb High-Protein Pizza Revolutions

Recipe 61: Grilled Chicken and Roasted Pepper Pizza

Savor the smoky grilled chicken and aromatic roasted peppers fusion with the "Grilled Chicken and Roasted Peppers Pizza." This masterpiece reimagines pizza by placing protein at its heart and reducing carbs. Dive into a revolution where traditional pizza gets a healthful, flavorful makeover.

Servings: 4

Prepping Time: 20 minutes

Cook Time: 15 minutes

Difficulty: Moderate

Ingredients:

- ✓ 1 low-carb pizza crust & 1 cup grilled chicken, thinly sliced

- ✓ 1/2 cup roasted bell peppers, sliced & 1/4 cup red onion, thinly sliced

- ✓ 3/4 cup mozzarella cheese, shredded
- ✓ 1/3 cup pizza sauce (low-carb, if desired) & 1 tsp dried oregano
- ✓ 1 tsp dried basil & Olive oil for drizzling & Salt and pepper to taste

Step-by-Step Preparation:

1. Preheat the oven as per the pizza crust's instructions.
2. Lay out the crust on a pizza stone or baking sheet.
3. Spread the pizza sauce evenly over the crust.
4. Sprinkle the cheese, followed by grilled chicken, roasted peppers, and red onion.
5. Season with oregano, basil, salt, and pepper.
6. Drizzle a bit of olive oil on top.
7. Bake as per crust instructions or until cheese is bubbly and golden.
8. Allow to cool for a few minutes before slicing.

Nutritional Facts: (Per serving)

- ➤ Calories: 310 kcal
- ➤ Protein: 22g
- ➤ Carbohydrates: 15g
- ➤ Dietary Fiber: 5g
- ➤ Sugars: 4g
- ➤ Fat: 18g
- ➤ Sodium: 450mg

Unveiling the modern transformation of the classic pizza - "Grilled Chicken and Roasted Pepper Pizza" champions a healthy twist without compromising flavor. Every bite offers a delightful crunch, rich cheesiness, and a burst of protein goodness. Perfect for those craving a pizza experience that aligns with their health-conscious goals. Indulge without guilt!

Recipe 62: Tart with Tomatoes, Basil, Salami, Black Olives

Experience a taste revolution with the "Tart with Tomatoes, Basil, Salami, and Black Olives." This unique spin on traditional pizza-style tarts promises robust flavors while being mindful of your carbs and protein. Indulge in this modern culinary creation that unites freshness with savory delight.

Servings: 6

Prepping Time: 25 minutes

Cook Time: 20 minutes

Difficulty: Moderate

Ingredients:

- ✓ 1 low-carb tart crust & 1 cup cherry tomatoes, halved
- ✓ 1/2 cup fresh basil leaves, torn & 1/3 cup salami slices, chopped
- ✓ 1/4 cup black olives, pitted and sliced & 1 cup mozzarella cheese, shredded
- ✓ 2 tbsp olive oil & 1 garlic clove, minced
- ✓ Salt and pepper to taste

Step-by-Step Preparation:

1. Preheat the oven according to the tart crust's instructions.

2. Roll out the crust into a sour pan.

3. In a bowl, mix olive oil and minced garlic. Brush this mixture over the cutting base.

4. Layer with shredded mozzarella, followed by cherry tomatoes, salami slices, and black olives.

5. Season with salt and pepper.

6. Bake until the crust turns golden and the cheese is bubbly approximately 20 minutes.

7. Garnish with torn fresh basil before serving.

Nutritional Facts: (Per serving)

➢ Calories: 280 kcal

➢ Protein: 12g

➢ Carbohydrates: 12g

➢ Dietary Fiber: 4g

➢ Sugars: 2g

➢ Fat: 20g

➢ Sodium: 520mg

Dive into the future of low-carb, high-protein delicacies with this outstanding tart. Each slice offers a harmonious blend of juicy tomatoes, aromatic basil, spicy salami, and salty olives. It's a taste journey that champions healthful eating without sacrificing the classic flavors we all adore. Let your pizza experience evolve!

Recipe 63: Mini Pizza Galette

Unleash a wave of culinary satisfaction with the "Mini Pizza Gillette." Designed for those who cherish flavor and health, this miniature delight fits perfectly into the low-carb, high-protein lifestyle. Relish the exquisite taste of pizza in a bite-sized form that's revolutionizing how we think about our favorite Italian dish.

Servings: 12 mini pizzas

Prepping Time: 20 minutes

Cook Time: 15 minutes

Difficulty: Easy

Ingredients:

- ✓ 1 low-carb pizza dough & 1/2 cup tomato sauce (low-sugar)
- ✓ 1 cup mozzarella cheese, shredded & 1/4 cup bell peppers, finely chopped
- ✓ 1/4 cup onions, finely chopped & 1/2 cup grilled chicken, diced
- ✓ 2 tbsp olive oil & Salt and pepper to taste
- ✓ Fresh basil for garnish

Step-by-Step Preparation:

1. Preheat oven to 400°F (200°C).

2. Roll out the pizza dough with a cookie cutter or cup to cut out mini pizza bases.

3. Place each mini base on a baking sheet.

4. Brush olive oil, spread a teaspoon of tomato sauce on each, and sprinkle with cheese.

5. Top with bell peppers, onions, and diced chicken.

6. Season with salt and pepper.

7. Bake for 12-15 minutes or until the edges are golden and the cheese is melted.

8. Garnish with fresh basil before serving.

Nutritional Facts: (Per serving)

➢ Calories: 90 kcal

➢ Protein: 7g

➢ Carbohydrates: 4g

➢ Dietary Fiber: 1g

➢ Sugars: 1g

➢ Fat: 6g

➢ Sodium: 140mg

Take a bite and travel to a world where nutrition meets classic pizza taste. "Mini Pizza Gillette" is not just a dish but an embodiment of the modern gastronomic movement. These minuscule treats are flavorful and are the future of guilt-free indulgence. Join the revolution, one mini pizza at a time!

Recipe 64: Healthy Assorted Pizza

Discover the revolution in pizza-making with the "Healthy Assorted Pizza." This pizza promises a rich experience without compromising health goals. Infused with the goodness of low-carb ingredients and high-quality proteins, it's a compelling and nourishing Italian masterpiece.

Servings: 8 slices

Prepping Time: 25 minutes

Cook Time: 20 minutes

Difficulty: Medium

Ingredients:

- ✓ 1 large low-carb pizza crust & 1/2 cup tomato sauce (low-sugar)
- ✓ 1 cup mozzarella cheese, shredded & 1/4 cup bell peppers, thinly sliced
- ✓ 1/4 cup mushrooms, sliced & 1/4 cup black olives, sliced
- ✓ 1/2 cup grilled chicken breast, sliced & 2 tbsp olive oil
- ✓ Fresh basil leaves for garnish & Salt and pepper to taste

Step-by-Step Preparation:

1. Preheat oven to 425°F (220°C).

2. Lay out the pizza crust on a pizza stone or baking sheet.

3. Evenly spread tomato sauce over the crust.

4. Sprinkle mozzarella cheese on top.

5. Arrange bell peppers, mushrooms, olives, and chicken slices over the cheese.

6. Drizzle with olive oil and season with salt and pepper.

7. Bake in the oven for 18-20 minutes or until the crust turns golden.

8. Garnish with fresh basil leaves before serving.

Nutritional Facts: (Per serving)

➢ Calories: 190 kcal

➢ Protein: 15g

➢ Carbohydrates: 8g

➢ Dietary Fiber: 2g

➢ Sugars: 2g

➢ Fat: 12g

➢ Sodium: 180mg

Experience the evolution of classic pizza with this health-focused twist. Every "Healthy Assorted Pizza" slice offers a burst of flavors without the carb overload. Dive into this guilt-free delight that's redefining pizza for the modern Embrace the new-age pizza revolution, one healthy slice at a time!

Recipe 65: BBQ Chicken Pizza Recipe

Indulge in the ultimate fusion of smoky barbecued chicken and classic pizza with the "BBQ Chicken Pizza Recipe." This low-carb, high-protein delight is a game changer in gourmet pizzas.

Servings: 8 slices

Prepping Time: 20 minutes

Cook Time: 18 minutes

Difficulty: Medium

Ingredients:

- ✓ 1 large low-carb pizza crust
- ✓ 1/2 cup BBQ sauce (low-sugar)
- ✓ 1 cup mozzarella cheese, shredded
- ✓ 1/2 cup BBQ chicken, cooked and shredded
- ✓ 1/4 cup red onions, thinly sliced
- ✓ 1/4 cup bell peppers, thinly sliced

✓ 1/4 cup cilantro, chopped

✓ 2 tbsp olive oil

Step-by-Step Preparation:

1. Preheat oven to 425°F (220°C).

2. Spread the pizza crust on a baking sheet or pizza stone.

3. Evenly apply BBQ sauce over the crust.

4. Sprinkle mozzarella cheese on top.

5. Scatter BBQ chicken, red onions, and bell peppers over the cheese.

6. Drizzle with olive oil.

7. Bake for 16-18 minutes or until the crust is golden and the cheese is bubbly.

8. Garnish with chopped cilantro before serving.

Nutritional Facts: (Per serving)

➢ Calories: 195 kcal

➢ Protein: 16g

➢ Carbohydrates: 9g

➢ Dietary Fiber: 2g

➢ Sugars: 3g

➢ Fat: 11g

➢ Sodium: 250mg

Elevate your pizza nights with the "BBQ Chicken Pizza Recipe," a harmonious blend of BBQ goodness and pizza's comforting charm. This dish promises an unforgettable culinary journey, offering a modern twist to the age-old pizza tradition. Embrace the pizza revolution, where flavor meets nutrition!

Recipe 66: Flatbread Pepperoni Pizza

Reimagine your classic pepperoni pizza with this "Flatbread Pepperoni Pizza" recipe. Light, crunchy, and packed with protein, this low-carb delight transforms your pizza experience into a healthier yet flavorful adventure, making it a standout in the pizza revolution.

Servings: 4

Prepping Time: 10 minutes

Cook Time: 12 minutes

Difficulty: Easy

Ingredients:

- ✓ 1 large low-carb flatbread
- ✓ 1/2 cup marinara sauce (low-sugar)
- ✓ 3/4 cup mozzarella cheese, shredded
- ✓ 1/4 cup pepperoni slices
- ✓ 1/4 cup black olives, sliced

- ✓ 1/4 teaspoon dried oregano
- ✓ 1/4 teaspoon red chili flakes (optional)
- ✓ Fresh basil leaves for garnish

Step-by-Step Preparation:

1. Preheat your oven to 400°F (200°C).
2. Lay the flatbread on a baking sheet.
3. Spread the marinara sauce evenly across the flatbread.
4. Sprinkle the shredded mozzarella over the sauce.
5. Arrange pepperoni slices and black olives on top.
6. Season with dried oregano and red chili flakes.
7. Bake for 10-12 minutes or until the cheese is melted and the flatbread is crispy.
8. Garnish with fresh basil leaves before serving.

Nutritional Facts: (Per serving)

- ➤ Calories: 210 kcal
- ➤ Protein: 14g
- ➤ Carbohydrates: 8g
- ➤ Dietary Fiber: 3g
- ➤ Sugars: 2g
- ➤ Fat: 15g
- ➤ Sodium: 370mg

Dive into a slice of this "Flatbread Pepperoni Pizza" and experience a harmonious blend of traditional flavors with a modern health-focused twist. It's the perfect testament to how indulgence and nutrition coexist in pizza. Celebrate the revolution one slice at a time!

Recipe 67: Protein-Packed Seafood Pizza

Savor the fusion of the sea's finest and the classic Italian dish with the "Protein-Packed Seafood Pizza." An emblem of the pizza revolution, this recipe amplifies the protein content while keeping carbs in check, promising flavor and fitness on a plate.

Servings: 4

Prepping Time: 15 minutes

Cook Time: 20 minutes

Difficulty: Intermediate

Ingredients:

- ✓ 1 large low-carb pizza crust
- ✓ 1/2 cup marinara sauce (low-sugar)
- ✓ 3/4 cup mozzarella cheese, shredded
- ✓ 1/2 cup assorted seafood (shrimps, clams, squid rings)
- ✓ 1/4 cup red bell pepper, sliced
- ✓ 1/4 cup green olives, sliced
- ✓ 1/4 teaspoon dried oregano & Fresh parsley for garnish

Step-by-Step Preparation:

1. Preheat the oven to 425°F (220°C).

2. Spread the marinara sauce evenly on the pizza crust.

3. Sprinkle the shredded mozzarella cheese.

4. Evenly distribute the assorted seafood, bell peppers, and olives on the pizza.

5. Season with dried oregano.

6. Bake for 18-20 minutes or until the seafood is cooked and the cheese is golden.

7. Garnish with fresh parsley before serving.

Nutritional Facts: (Per serving)

➤ Calories: 230 kcal

➤ Protein: 19g

➤ Carbohydrates: 10g

➤ Dietary Fiber: 3g

➤ Sugars: 3g

➤ Fat: 12g

➤ Sodium: 390mg

Unveil a new dimension of pizza with the "Protein-Packed Seafood Pizza." It's where the ocean's treasures meet the comforting embrace of cheesy goodness. This creation proves that a protein-packed meal can be both sumptuous and satisfying, reshaping the narrative of healthy eating. Enjoy!

Recipe 68: Supreme Pizza Lifted Slice

Experience a culinary delight with the "Supreme Pizza Lifted Slice." This pizza showcases the ideal merger of taste and health. Perfect for fitness enthusiasts with a penchant for gourmet.

Servings: 8 slices

Prepping Time: 20 minutes

Cook Time: 25 minutes

Difficulty: Intermediate

Ingredients:

- ✓ 1 large low-carb pizza crust
- ✓ 1/2 cup marinara sauce (low-sugar)
- ✓ 1 cup mozzarella cheese, shredded
- ✓ 1/2 cup diced chicken breast, cooked
- ✓ 1/4 cup bell peppers, mixed colors, sliced
- ✓ 1/4 cup red onions, sliced

- ✓ 2 tablespoons black olives, sliced
- ✓ 1/4 cup mushrooms, sliced
- ✓ Fresh basil leaves for garnish

Step-by-Step Preparation:

1. Preheat the oven to 425°F (220°C).
2. Evenly spread the marinara sauce on the pizza crust.
3. Sprinkle the shredded mozzarella cheese.
4. Top with chicken, bell peppers, red onions, olives, and mushrooms.
5. Bake for 22-25 minutes or until the cheese is bubbly and golden.
6. Garnish with fresh basil leaves before serving.

Nutritional Facts: (Per serving)

- ➢ Calories: 210 kcal
- ➢ Protein: 18g
- ➢ Carbohydrates: 8g
- ➢ Dietary Fiber: 2g
- ➢ Sugars: 3g
- ➢ Fat: 10g
- ➢ Sodium: 370mg

Indulging in the "Supreme Pizza Lifted Slice" is a sensory treat. Bursting with flavors and packed with protein, it's the epitome of modern gourmet dining, offering the best of nutrition and indulgence in every bite. Enjoy the revolution on your plate!

Recipe 69: Home-made Vegan Pizza

Dive into the world of healthy indulgence with the "Home-made Vegan Pizza." This low-carb, high-protein masterpiece celebrates the richness of plant-based ingredients, offering a perfect blend of nutrition and flavor. Elevate your pizza nights with this vegan delight!

Servings: 8 slices

Prepping Time: 30 minutes

Cook Time: 20 minutes

Difficulty: Intermediate

Ingredients:

- ✓ 1 large low-carb vegan pizza crust
- ✓ 1/2 cup vegan marinara sauce
- ✓ 1 cup vegan mozzarella cheese, shredded
- ✓ 1/4 cup cherry tomatoes, halved
- ✓ 1/4 cup red bell peppers, sliced
- ✓ 1/4 cup black olives, sliced
- ✓ 1/4 cup red onions, thinly sliced

- ✓ 2 tablespoons nutritional yeast (for added protein)
- ✓ Fresh basil leaves for garnish

Step-by-Step Preparation:

1. Preheat the oven to 425°F (220°C).
2. Spread the vegan marinara sauce evenly on the pizza crust.
3. Sprinkle the vegan mozzarella cheese generously.
4. Top with cherry tomatoes, red bell peppers, olives, and red onions.
5. Sprinkle nutritional yeast over the toppings.
6. Bake for 18-20 minutes or until the cheese melts and turns golden.
7. Garnish with fresh basil leaves before serving.

Nutritional Facts: (Per serving)

- ➤ Calories: 180 kcal
- ➤ Protein: 12g
- ➤ Carbohydrates: 9g
- ➤ Dietary Fiber: 3g
- ➤ Sugars: 2g
- ➤ Fat: 9g
- ➤ Sodium: 290mg

Crafted for the discerning vegan palate, the "Home-made Vegan Pizza" embodies the spirit of gourmet health food. With every slice rich in protein and low in carbs, this pizza ensures that your taste buds and fitness goals are equally catered to. Bon appétit!

Recipe 70: Buffalo Chicken Pizza

Savor the spicy twist of the "Buffalo Chicken Pizza," a dish that combines classic pizza charm with the zest of buffalo chicken. With high protein and low carbs, this dish brings a bold flavor profile for a transformative pizza experience.

Servings: 8 slices

Prepping Time: 25 minutes

Cook Time: 20 minutes

Difficulty: Intermediate

Ingredients:

- ✓ 1 large low-carb pizza crust
- ✓ 1/2 cup buffalo sauce
- ✓ 1 cup mozzarella cheese, shredded
- ✓ 1/2 cup cooked chicken breast, shredded
- ✓ 1/4 cup red onions, thinly sliced

- ✓ 1/4 cup blue cheese crumbles

- ✓ 2 green onions, chopped

- ✓ 1/4 cup celery, finely diced

- ✓ Fresh cilantro leaves for garnish

Step-by-Step Preparation:

1. Preheat the oven to 425°F (220°C).

2. Spread the buffalo sauce evenly over the pizza crust.

3. Sprinkle mozzarella cheese over the sauce.

4. Top with shredded chicken, red onions, blue cheese crumbles, green onions, and celery.

5. Bake for 18-20 minutes or until cheese is bubbly and golden.

6. Garnish with fresh cilantro leaves before slicing and serving.

Nutritional Facts: (Per serving)

- ➢ Calories: 190 kcal

- ➢ Protein: 14g

- ➢ Carbohydrates: 10g

- ➢ Dietary Fiber: 2g

- ➢ Sugars: 1g

- ➢ Fat: 10g

- ➢ Sodium: 350mg

Lift your pizza game to new culinary heights with the "Buffalo Chicken Pizza." Each slice promises a whirlwind of flavors, ensuring every bite perfectly balances spicy, creamy, and cheesy goodness. Dive into this modern classic!

Chapter 08: High Protein Fish Delicacies

←—————————————————————————→

Recipe 71: Teriyaki Salmon Skewers

Embark on a flavorful journey with "Teriyaki Salmon Skewers," a high-protein fish delicacy that infuses teriyaki's sweet and savory notes into succulent salmon. Perfect for grilling enthusiasts, this dish brings the essence of Japanese cuisine to your plate.

Servings: 4

Prepping Time: 20 minutes (+1-hour marinating)

Cook Time: 10 minutes

Difficulty: Easy

Ingredients:

- ✓ 4 salmon fillets cut into 1-inch cubes & 1/2 cup teriyaki sauce

- ✓ 1 tablespoon sesame oil & 1 tablespoon honey

- ✓ 1 garlic clove, minced & 1 tablespoon fresh ginger, grated

- ✓ 1 tablespoon sesame seeds
- ✓ 1 green onion, finely chopped for garnish

Step-by-Step Preparation:

1. Combine teriyaki sauce, sesame oil, honey, garlic, and ginger in a bowl. Mix well.

2. Add salmon cubes to the mixture, ensuring they're well-coated. Marinate for at least 1 hour in the refrigerator.

3. Preheat the grill to medium-high heat.

4. Thread marinated salmon cubes onto skewers.

5. Grill 4-5 minutes on each side or until the salmon is cooked.

6. Sprinkle with sesame seeds and green onions before serving.

Nutritional Facts: (Per serving)

- ➢ Calories: 280 kcal
- ➢ Protein: 25g
- ➢ Carbohydrates: 15g
- ➢ Dietary Fiber: 0.5g
- ➢ Sugars: 12g
- ➢ Fat: 12g
- ➢ Sodium: 780mg

Dive into the harmonious blend of sweet and savory with these "Teriyaki Salmon Skewers." Whether hosting a backyard BBQ or simply craving a taste of Japan, this dish promises a memorable culinary experience with every bite.

Recipe 72: Grilled Salmon Burger

Introduce your taste buds to the "Grilled Salmon Burger," a High Protein Fish Delicacy that merges the heartiness of a burger with the richness of salmon. Savor the tender, flavorful fish patty while relishing the classic burger experience.

Servings: 4

Prepping Time: 25 minutes

Cook Time: 10 minutes

Difficulty: Moderate

Ingredients:

- ✓ 1-pound fresh salmon fillet, skin removed
- ✓ 1/4 cup breadcrumbs
- ✓ 1 large egg, lightly beaten
- ✓ 2 tablespoons fresh dill, chopped
- ✓ 1 tablespoon lemon zest

- ✓ 1/4 cup mayonnaise
- ✓ Salt and pepper to taste
- ✓ 4 whole grain buns
- ✓ Lettuce, tomato slices, and red onion for garnish

Step-by-Step Preparation:

1. In a food processor, pulse salmon until finely chopped but not pureed.

2. Transfer to a bowl and mix with breadcrumbs, egg, dill, lemon zest, mayonnaise, salt, and pepper.

3. Form into 4 patties.

4. Preheat the grill to medium heat. Oil the grill grate.

5. Grill patties for 4-5 minutes per side or until cooked through.

6. Serve on buns with lettuce, tomato, and onion.

Nutritional Facts: (Per serving)

- ➤ Calories: 345 kcal
- ➤ Protein: 32g
- ➤ Carbohydrates: 26g
- ➤ Dietary Fiber: 3g
- ➤ Sugars: 4g
- ➤ Fat: 12g
- ➤ Sodium: 580mg

Elevate your traditional burger game with the "Grilled Salmon Burger." Packed with protein and bursting with flavors, it's a gourmet twist on a classic that's both nourishing and incredibly satisfying.

Recipe 73: Juicy Cheese

Embark on a culinary adventure with "Juicy Cheese," a surprising fusion of High Protein Fish Delicacies. Experience the creaminess of cheese combined with the savory notes of fish, offering an unexpected delight.

Servings: 4

Prepping Time: 20 minutes

Cook Time: 15 minutes

Difficulty: Moderate

Ingredients:

- ✓ 4 fillets of white fish (e.g., cod or tilapia)
- ✓ 4 slices of aged cheddar cheese
- ✓ 2 tablespoons olive oil
- ✓ Salt and pepper to taste
- ✓ 1 teaspoon garlic powder
- ✓ 1 teaspoon onion powder
- ✓ Fresh dill for garnish & Lemon wedges for serving

Step-by-Step Preparation:

1. Preheat the oven to 400°F (200°C).

2. Season fish fillets with salt, pepper, garlic powder, and onion powder.

3. In a skillet, heat olive oil over medium heat. Sear fish fillets for 2 minutes on each side.

4. Transfer the fish to an oven-safe dish.

5. Place a slice of cheese on each fillet.

6. Bake in the oven for 10-12 minutes until the cheese is melted and the fish flakes easily.

7. Garnish with fresh dill and serve with lemon wedges.

Nutritional Facts: (Per serving)

- Calories: 290 kcal

- Protein: 28g

- Carbohydrates: 1g

- Dietary Fiber: 0g

- Sugars: 0g

- Fat: 18g

- Sodium: 250mg

Venture beyond the ordinary with "Juicy Cheese." This dish is a testament to the magic that happens when the melt-in-your-mouth texture of cheese meets the fish's tenderness. A true delicacy for the daring palate!

Recipe 74: Lavish on The Grill with Juicy Cheese

Indulge in a tantalizing culinary creation with "Lavish on The Grill with Juicy Cheese." This high-protein fish delicacy merges the smokiness of grilled fish with the lushness of melty cheese, ensuring every bite is an exquisite experience.

Servings: 4

Prepping Time: 15 minutes

Cook Time: 20 minutes

Difficulty: Intermediate

Ingredients:

- ✓ 4 fillets of white fish (e.g., halibut or sea bass)
- ✓ 4 slices of rich gouda cheese
- ✓ 2 tablespoons of olive oil
- ✓ Salt and freshly ground black pepper to taste
- ✓ 2 teaspoons fresh thyme, chopped

- ✓ 1 tablespoon lemon zest
- ✓ Fresh parsley for garnish
- ✓ Lemon wedges for serving

Step-by-Step Preparation:

1. Preheat the grill to medium-high heat.

2. Rub each fish fillet with olive oil, then season with salt, pepper, thyme, and lemon zest.

3. Place fish on the grill and cook for 5-7 minutes on each side or until nearly done.

4. Top each fillet with a slice of gouda cheese and close the grill lid. Cook for another 2-3 minutes or until the cheese is melted.

5. Transfer fish to serving plates and garnish with fresh parsley. Serve with lemon wedges.

Nutritional Facts: (Per serving)

- ➢ Calories: 315 kcal
- ➢ Protein: 30g
- ➢ Carbohydrates: 1g
- ➢ Dietary Fiber: 0g
- ➢ Sugars: 0g
- ➢ Fat: 21g
- ➢ Sodium: 320mg

Experience the brilliance of "Lavish on The Grill with Juicy Cheese," where the contrast of flavors and textures elevates your dining affair. It's not just a dish; it's a celebration of gourmet mastery!

Recipe 75: Smoky Salmon Pizza

Savor the rich fusion of smoked salmon on a crispy crust with the "Smoky Salmon Pizza." This high-protein fish delicacy combines traditional pizza charm with the elegance of salmon, promising an unmatched gastronomic experience.

Servings: 4

Prepping Time: 20 minutes

Cook Time: 15 minutes

Difficulty: Moderate

Ingredients:

- ✓ 1 ready-made pizza crust
- ✓ 200g smoked salmon slices
- ✓ 100g cream cheese, softened
- ✓ 2 tablespoons fresh dill, chopped
- ✓ 1 small red onion, thinly sliced
- ✓ 1 tablespoon capers

- ✓ 1 tablespoon olive oil
- ✓ Freshly ground black pepper to taste
- ✓ Lemon wedges for serving

Step-by-Step Preparation:

1. Preheat the oven as per the pizza crust instructions.
2. Roll out the pizza crust on a baking tray and brush with olive oil.
3. Evenly spread the softened cream cheese over the crust.
4. Bake in the oven until the crust is golden and crispy.
5. Remove from oven and immediately top with smoked salmon slices, red onion, capers, and fresh dill.
6. Season with freshly ground black pepper.
7. Slice and serve with lemon wedges.

Nutritional Facts: (Per serving)

- ➤ Calories: 390 kcal
- ➤ Protein: 22g
- ➤ Carbohydrates: 45g
- ➤ Dietary Fiber: 2g
- ➤ Sugars: 3g
- ➤ Fat: 15g
- ➤ Sodium: 720mg

Embrace the sophistication of the "Smoky Salmon Pizza," where every slice tantalizes the palate with a delightful blend of flavors. Perfect for both casual gatherings and gourmet dinners!

Recipe 76: Salmon Fried Rice with Pickled Egg

Dive into the robust flavors of "Salmon Fried Rice with Pickled Egg." This dish marries the umami-rich taste of salmon with the tanginess of pickled eggs, offering a high-protein, unique culinary delight.

Servings: 4

Prepping Time: 20 minutes

Cook Time: 20 minutes

Difficulty: Moderate

Ingredients:

- ✓ 250g cooked salmon, flaked

- ✓ 2 cups cooked rice

- ✓ 2 pickled eggs, diced

- ✓ 3 green onions, sliced

- ✓ 2 cloves garlic, minced

- ✓ 2 tablespoons soy sauce
- ✓ 1 tablespoon sesame oil
- ✓ 1 cup mixed vegetables (peas, carrots, bell peppers)
- ✓ Freshly ground black pepper to taste
- ✓ 1 tablespoon olive oil for frying

Step-by-Step Preparation:

1. In a large skillet, heat olive oil over medium heat. Sauté garlic until fragrant.
2. Add the mixed vegetables and cook until tender.
3. Add the cooked rice, stirring frequently to avoid sticking.
4. Stir in flaked salmon and diced pickled eggs.
5. Drizzle soy sauce and sesame oil, mixing well.
6. Finish with green onions and season with black pepper.
7. Serve hot.

Nutritional Facts: (Per serving)

- ➢ Calories: 380 kcal
- ➢ Protein: 25g
- ➢ Carbohydrates: 45g
- ➢ Dietary Fiber: 3g
- ➢ Sugars: 2g
- ➢ Fat: 12g
- ➢ Sodium: 650mg

Relish a "Salmon Fried Rice with Pickled Egg" bowl and experience a delightful blend of textures and flavors. This dish is an adventurous take on traditional fried rice that will excite your taste buds.

Recipe 77: Wagyu Beef Sushi - Japanese Food

They are introducing "Wagyu Beef Sushi," a culinary delight where Japanese finesse meets luxury. Relish the buttery texture of Wagyu beef paired with traditional sushi rice for a protein-packed gastronomic journey.

Servings: 4

Prepping Time: 30 minutes

Cook Time: 10 minutes

Difficulty: Advanced

Ingredients:

- ✓ 200g Wagyu beef, thinly sliced
- ✓ 2 cups sushi rice, cooked and seasoned
- ✓ 1 sheet nori (seaweed)
- ✓ Wasabi and soy sauce for serving
- ✓ 1 tablespoon sesame seeds, toasted
- ✓ Pickled ginger

Step-by-Step Preparation:

1. Cook sushi rice as per packet instructions and season with sushi vinegar.

2. On a sushi mat, lay out the nori sheet. Gently press a layer of sushi rice onto the nori.

3. Place a slice of Wagyu beef over the rice.

4. Roll the sushi using the mat, ensuring a tight roll.

5. Slice the roll into bite-sized pieces.

6. Serve with wasabi, soy sauce, and pickled ginger.

Nutritional Facts: (Per serving)

- Calories: 340 kcal

- Protein: 24g

- Carbohydrates: 40g

- Dietary Fiber: 1g

- Sugars: 1g

- Fat: 10g

- Sodium: 250mg

Experience the luxury of "Wagyu Beef Sushi," a dish that harmoniously merges the richness of Wagyu with the simplicity of sushi. Perfect for special occasions or when you're in the mood for a high-end treat.

Recipe 78: Barbeque Grill of Meat

Dive into a rich, smoky world with the "Barbeque Grill of Meat", where every bite brings forth an explosion of flavors. Whether you're hosting a summer gathering or looking for a protein-packed meal, this dish is sure to please.

Servings: 4

Prepping Time: 20 minutes

Cook Time: 40 minutes

Difficulty: Intermediate

Ingredients:

- ✓ 500g mixed meat (chicken, beef, lamb)
- ✓ 2 tablespoons olive oil
- ✓ 3 garlic cloves, minced
- ✓ 1 tablespoon paprika
- ✓ Salt and pepper to taste

✓ Fresh rosemary and thyme

✓ Barbeque sauce for basting and serving

Step-by-Step Preparation:

1. In a bowl, mix olive oil, garlic, paprika, salt, pepper, rosemary, and thyme.

2. Marinate the meats with the prepared mixture and refrigerate for at least 2 hours.

3. Preheat the grill on medium-high heat.

4. Place the marinated meats on the grill, turning occasionally and basting with barbeque sauce.

5. Grill until the meat is cooked to your desired level of doneness.

6. Serve hot with extra barbeque sauce.

Nutritional Facts: (Per serving)

➢ Calories: 350 kcal

➢ Protein: 28g

➢ Carbohydrates: 5g

➢ Dietary Fiber: 1g

➢ Sugars: 3g

➢ Fat: 24g

➢ Sodium: 450mg

Relish the irresistible aroma and flavors of the "Barbeque Grill of Meat". Ideal for outdoor events, it promises a memorable dining experience with each tender and flavorful bite. Enjoy this high-protein delicacy!

Recipe 79: Puff Pastry Pinwheels Stuffed

Savor the rich, flaky goodness of "Puff Pastry Pinwheels Stuffed" with protein-rich seafood filling. A perfect blend of crispy pastry and sumptuous filling, these pinwheels are a seafood lover's dream appetizer.

Servings: 6

Prepping Time: 25 minutes

Cook Time: 15 minutes

Difficulty: Intermediate

Ingredients:

- ✓ 1 sheet puff pastry, thawed
- ✓ 200g mixed seafood (shrimp, crab, scallops), finely chopped
- ✓ 2 tablespoons cream cheese
- ✓ 1 tablespoon fresh dill, chopped
- ✓ 1 garlic clove, minced
- ✓ Salt and pepper to taste & 1 egg, beaten (for egg wash)

Step-by-Step Preparation:

1. Preheat the oven to 400°F (200°C).

2. Roll out the puff pastry sheet on a lightly floured surface.

3. Combine seafood, cream cheese, dill, garlic, salt, and pepper in a bowl.

4. Spread the mixture evenly over the puff pastry.

5. Roll the pastry tightly into a log.

6. Slice the log into pinwheels, place on a baking sheet, and brush with egg wash.

7. Bake for 15 minutes or until golden brown.

Nutritional Facts: (Per serving)

➢ Calories: 280 kcal

➢ Protein: 12g

➢ Carbohydrates: 18g

➢ Dietary Fiber: 0.5g

➢ Sugars: 1g

➢ Fat: 18g

➢ Sodium: 220mg

The "Puff Pastry Pinwheels Stuffed" offers a delightful twist to traditional seafood appetizers. Experience a bite of the ocean with each flaky piece, ensuring a memorable gastronomic journey that leaves you craving more.

Recipe 80: BBQ Cutlets on Rustic

Indulge in the savory sensation of "BBQ Cutlets on Rustic." This fish delicacy offers a unique blend of smoky barbecue flavors and the succulence of prime fish cutlets, delivering a culinary experience that's both rustic and refined.

Servings: 4

Prepping Time: 20 minutes

Cook Time: 15 minutes

Difficulty: Intermediate

Ingredients:

- ✓ 4 fish cutlets (such as salmon or tuna)
- ✓ 3 tablespoons BBQ sauce
- ✓ 2 teaspoons olive oil
- ✓ 1 garlic clove, minced
- ✓ Salt and pepper to taste

✓ Fresh herbs (like rosemary and thyme) for garnishing

Step-by-Step Preparation:

1. Preheat the grill to medium-high heat.

2. Rub fish cutlets with olive oil, garlic, salt, and pepper.

3. Place cutlets on the grill and cook on each side for 6-7 minutes or until the desired doneness.

4. Brush BBQ sauce generously over the fish during the last 2 minutes of grilling.

5. Remove from grill, garnish with fresh herbs.

Nutritional Facts: (Per serving)

➢ Calories: 260 kcal

➢ Protein: 25g

➢ Carbohydrates: 5g

➢ Dietary Fiber: 0.2g

➢ Sugars: 3g

➢ Fat: 15g

➢ Sodium: 320mg

Savor the richness of "BBQ Cutlets on Rustic," where the simplicity of grilling meets gourmet fish preparations. It's an epicurean delight promising a smoky and flavorful journey with every bite.

Chapter 09: High Protein Veggie Twists

Recipe 81: Black Bean and Quinoa Stuffed Bell Peppers

Discover the fusion of flavors in "Black Bean and Quinoa Stuffed Bell Peppers." This dish encapsulates nutrition and taste, combining the protein-rich goodness of black beans and quinoa with the fresh crunch of bell peppers.

Servings: 4

Prepping Time: 20 minutes

Cook Time: 25 minutes

Difficulty: Intermediate

Ingredients:

- ✓ 4 large bell peppers (various colors) & 1 cup cooked quinoa

- ✓ 1 cup cooked black beans & 1/2 cup diced tomatoes

- ✓ 1/4 cup diced onions & 2 cloves garlic, minced
- ✓ 1 teaspoon cumin & Salt and pepper to taste
- ✓ Olive oil for drizzling & Fresh cilantro for garnishing

Step-by-Step Preparation:

1. Preheat oven to 375°F.
2. Cut the tops off the bell peppers and remove the seeds.
3. Combine quinoa, black beans, tomatoes, onions, garlic, cumin, salt, and pepper in a mixing bowl.
4. Stuff each bell pepper with the quinoa and black bean mixture.
5. Place the stuffed peppers in a baking dish, drizzle with olive oil.
6. Bake for 25 minutes or until the peppers are tender.
7. Garnish with fresh cilantro before serving.

Nutritional Facts: (Per serving)

- ➤ Calories: 210 kcal
- ➤ Protein: 9g
- ➤ Carbohydrates: 39g
- ➤ Dietary Fiber: 8g
- ➤ Sugars: 6g
- ➤ Fat: 2.5g
- ➤ Sodium: 15mg

Relish the vibrant hues and hearty textures of "Black Bean and Quinoa Stuffed Bell Peppers." A delightful addition to your High Protein Veggie Twists collection, these peppers promise health and gastronomic satisfaction.

Recipe 82: Hummus Toasts with Tomatoes

Elevate your breakfast game with "Hummus Toasts with Tomatoes." This simple yet delightful dish combines the creamy texture of hummus with the fresh tang of tomatoes, offering a protein-packed start to your day.

Servings: 4

Prepping Time: 10 minutes

Cook Time: 5 minutes

Difficulty: Easy

Ingredients:

- ✓ 4 slices whole grain bread
- ✓ 1 cup hummus (store-bought or homemade)
- ✓ 2 ripe tomatoes, sliced thinly
- ✓ Olive oil for drizzling
- ✓ Salt and pepper to taste
- ✓ Fresh basil leaves for garnish (optional)

Step-by-Step Preparation:

1. Toast the bread slices until golden brown.

2. Evenly spread hummus on each toast.

3. Arrange tomato slices on top of the hummus.

4. Drizzle with a touch of olive oil and sprinkle with salt and pepper.

5. Garnish with basil leaves if desired.

Nutritional Facts: (Per serving)

➤ Calories: 230 kcal

➤ Protein: 9g

➤ Carbohydrates: 32g

➤ Dietary Fiber: 8g

➤ Sugars: 4g

➤ Fat: 9g

➤ Sodium: 310mg

Step into a world where simplicity meets flavor with "Hummus Toasts with Tomatoes." Ideal for breakfast or a quick snack, this dish not only pleases the palate but also aligns with your health goals. Enjoy your High Protein Veggie Twists journey!

Recipe 83: Cheese Tortellini, Italian Sausage

Indulge in the rich flavors of Italy with the "Cheese Tortellini, Italian Sausage" dish. This heartwarming combination of cheese-stuffed pasta and savory sausage is a testament to comfort food that's both delicious and protein-rich.

Servings: 4

Prepping Time: 15 minutes

Cook Time: 20 minutes

Difficulty: Medium

Ingredients:

- ✓ 2 cups cheese tortellini
- ✓ 4 Italian sausages, sliced
- ✓ 1 tbsp olive oil
- ✓ 2 garlic cloves, minced
- ✓ 1/2 cup diced tomatoes

- ✓ 1/2 cup grated Parmesan cheese
- ✓ Fresh basil for garnish
- ✓ Salt and pepper to taste

Step-by-Step Preparation:

1. Cook the tortellini according to package instructions; drain and set aside.

2. In a skillet, heat olive oil over medium heat. Add the sausage slices and cook until browned.

3. Add garlic and diced tomatoes to the skillet; sauté for a few minutes.

4. Combine the cooked tortellini with the sausage mixture.

5. Sprinkle with Parmesan cheese and season with salt and pepper.

6. Garnish with fresh basil leaves before serving.

Nutritional Facts: (Per serving)

- ➤ Calories: 480 kcal
- ➤ Protein: 25g
- ➤ Carbohydrates: 40g
- ➤ Dietary Fiber: 3g
- ➤ Sugars: 5g
- ➤ Fat: 25g
- ➤ Sodium: 710mg

Relish in the classic Italian flavors in the "Cheese Tortellini, Italian Sausage" dish. This harmonious blend of cheesy pasta and succulent sausage guarantees satisfaction in every bite, making it a staple in the High Protein Veggie Twists repertoire. Boon Appetite!

Recipe 84: Moroccan Spiced Chickpea Salad

Dive into a burst of exotic flavors with the "Moroccan Spiced Chickpea Salad." A delightful medley of protein-rich chickpeas, vibrant vegetables, and aromatic spices, this dish promises a compelling journey for your taste buds.

Servings: 4

Prepping Time: 15 minutes

Cook Time: 0 minutes (No cooking required)

Difficulty: Easy

Ingredients:

- ✓ 2 cups cooked chickpeas, drained
- ✓ 1 red bell pepper, diced
- ✓ 1 cucumber, diced
- ✓ 1/2 red onion, finely chopped
- ✓ 1/4 cup fresh cilantro, chopped
- ✓ 2 tbsp olive oil

- ✓ 1 tbsp lemon juice
- ✓ 2 tsp ground cumin
- ✓ 1 tsp paprika
- ✓ Salt and pepper to taste

Step-by-Step Preparation:

1. Combine chickpeas, bell pepper, cucumber, and red onion in a large bowl.

2. Whisk together olive oil, lemon juice, cumin, paprika, salt, and pepper in a separate small bowl to create the dressing.

3. Pour the dressing over the chickpea mixture and toss to coat evenly.

4. Garnish with fresh cilantro before serving.

Nutritional Facts: (Per serving)

- ➤ Calories: 210 kcal
- ➤ Protein: 8g
- ➤ Carbohydrates: 28g
- ➤ Dietary Fiber: 7g
- ➤ Sugars: 6g
- ➤ Fat: 9g
- ➤ Sodium: 70mg

Experience the magic of Moroccan cuisine in the comfort of your home with this "Moroccan Spiced Chickpea Salad." A protein-packed delight, it's perfect for those seeking nutrition and a culinary adventure in a High Protein Veggie Twists dish. Enjoy!

Recipe 85: Quinoa Salad with Green Beans

Introducing "Quinoa Salad with Green Beans," a symphony of fresh green beans and protein-rich quinoa brought together to create a nutritious and flavorful dish.

Servings: 4

Prepping Time: 20 minutes

Cook Time: 15 minutes

Difficulty: Easy

Ingredients:

- ✓ 1 cup cooked quinoa
- ✓ 1.5 cups green beans, trimmed and halved
- ✓ 1/2 cup cherry tomatoes, halved
- ✓ 1/4 cup feta cheese, crumbled
- ✓ 2 tbsp olive oil
- ✓ 1 tbsp lemon juice

✓ Salt and pepper to taste

✓ Fresh mint leaves for garnish

Step-by-Step Preparation:

1. Cook quinoa as per package instructions and let it cool.

2. Boil green beans in salted water until tender-crisp. Drain and cool.

3. Combine quinoa, green beans, and cherry tomatoes in a large bowl.

4. Drizzle with olive oil and lemon juice, and toss.

5. Season with salt and pepper, and sprinkle with feta cheese.

6. Garnish with fresh mint leaves before serving.

Nutritional Facts: (Per serving)

➤ Calories: 220 kcal

➤ Protein: 8g

➤ Carbohydrates: 31g

➤ Dietary Fiber: 5g

➤ Sugars: 3g

➤ Fat: 8g

➤ Sodium: 180mg

Dive into a delightful culinary journey with "Quinoa Salad with Green Beans." This High Protein, Veggie Twists recipe, is perfect for health enthusiasts looking for a tasty and nutritious treat. Enjoy your meal!

Recipe 86: Stew Vegetables and Legumes

Savor the rich textures and flavors of "Stew Vegetables and Legumes," an exquisite blend that merges the wholesomeness of veggies with the protein-packed goodness of legumes. An epitome of hearty and healthy!

Servings: 4

Prepping Time: 25 minutes

Cook Time: 40 minutes

Difficulty: Moderate

Ingredients:

- ✓ 1 cup chickpeas, soaked overnight
- ✓ 2 carrots, diced
- ✓ 1 zucchini, diced
- ✓ 2 potatoes, cubed
- ✓ 1 onion, finely chopped
- ✓ 2 cloves garlic, minced

- ✓ 1 can diced tomatoes
- ✓ 4 cups vegetable broth
- ✓ 1 tsp paprika
- ✓ Salt and pepper to taste
- ✓ 2 tbsp olive oil

Step-by-Step Preparation:

1. In a large pot, heat olive oil and sauté onion and garlic until translucent.

2. Add carrots, zucchini, and potatoes, cooking for 5 minutes.

3. Incorporate chickpeas, diced tomatoes, paprika, salt, and pepper.

4. Pour in vegetable broth, boil, then lower heat to simmer for 30-35 minutes.

5. Taste and adjust seasoning as needed before serving.

Nutritional Facts: (Per serving)

- ➤ Calories: 270 kcal
- ➤ Protein: 10g
- ➤ Carbohydrates: 46g
- ➤ Dietary Fiber: 11g
- ➤ Sugars: 8g
- ➤ Fat: 7g
- ➤ Sodium: 750mg

Unveil the union of delectable veggies and legumes with this "Stew Vegetables and Legumes" dish. Every spoonful promises a delightful burst of flavors, perfectly complementing your High Protein Veggie Twists culinary adventures. Cheers to nutritious feasting!

Recipe 87: Burrito Mexican Food

Embrace the vibrant flavors of Mexico with the "Burrito Mexican Food" dish. A fusion of wholesome veggies, protein-rich fillings, and zesty spices, this burrito is your ticket to a culinary fiesta, the veggie twist way!

Servings: 4

Prepping Time: 20 minutes

Cook Time: 25 minutes

Difficulty: Moderate

Ingredients:

- ✓ 4 large whole wheat tortillas & 1 cup cooked black beans
- ✓ 1 cup quinoa, cooked & 1 avocado, sliced
- ✓ 1 red bell pepper, diced & 1 onion, finely chopped
- ✓ 2 cloves garlic, minced & 1 cup lettuce, shredded
- ✓ 1/2 cup fresh salsa & 1 tsp ground cumin
- ✓ Salt and pepper to taste & 2 tbsp olive oil

Step-by-Step Preparation:

1. In a skillet, heat olive oil and sauté onions and garlic until translucent.

2. Add bell pepper, black beans, and cumin. Cook for 5 minutes.

3. Lay out tortillas and spread quinoa, bean mixture, avocado slices, lettuce, and salsa.

4. Season with salt and pepper.

5. Roll up the tortillas tightly, tucking in sides as you go.

Nutritional Facts: (Per serving)

➢ Calories: 350 kcal

➢ Protein: 12g

➢ Carbohydrates: 50g

➢ Dietary Fiber: 10g

➢ Sugars: 4g

➢ Fat: 15g

➢ Sodium: 500mg

With the "Burrito Mexican Food" dish, you're not just biting into a wrap but an experience. A harmonious blend of taste, texture, and nutrition, this burrito serves as a testament to the rich essence of Mexican cuisine, amplified with a high-protein veggie twist. Enjoy your meal!

Recipe 88: Meatballs, Spicy Stewed Chickpeas

Dive into a savory fusion of hearty meatballs paired with stewed chickpeas' rich, spicy goodness. This dish, "Meatballs, Spicy Stewed Chickpeas," effortlessly marries carnivorous cravings with legume love, all under the high protein veggie twist umbrella.

Servings: 4

Prepping Time: 15 minutes

Cook Time: 30 minutes

Difficulty: Moderate

Ingredients:

- ✓ 500g ground beef or turkey & 1 can (400g) chickpeas, drained and rinsed

- ✓ 1 onion, finely chopped & 2 cloves garlic, minced

- ✓ 1 can (400g) diced tomatoes & 1 tsp smoked paprika

- ✓ 1/2 tsp chili flakes & 2 tbsp olive oil

- ✓ Salt and pepper to taste

- ✓ Fresh parsley, chopped (for garnish)

Step-by-Step Preparation:

1. Form meat into small meatballs and set aside.

2. In a large pot, heat olive oil and sauté onions and garlic until translucent.

3. Add diced tomatoes, smoked paprika, and chili flakes. Simmer for 10 minutes.

4. Gently add the meatballs and chickpeas to the stew. Cook for 20 minutes or until meatballs are fully cooked.

5. Season with salt and pepper, and garnish with fresh parsley before serving.

Nutritional Facts: (Per serving)

➢ Calories: 420 kcal

➢ Protein: 25g

➢ Carbohydrates: 28g

➢ Dietary Fiber: 7g

➢ Sugars: 6g

➢ Fat: 25g

➢ Sodium: 500mg

"Meatballs, Spicy Stewed Chickpeas" is a culinary journey of contrasts. The juiciness of meatballs harmonizes beautifully with the robustness of chickpeas, offering a dish that's as nourishing as it is flavorful. Perfect for those nights when you yearn for comfort with a protein-packed veggie-twist punch!

Recipe 89: Thai Noodles with Boiled Pork

Indulge in the aromatic allure of "Thai Noodles with Boiled Pork," a dish that merges succulent pork's richness with fresh veggies' lightness. This high-protein recipe with a veggie twist promises a delicious journey through Thai flavors.

Servings: 4

Prepping Time: 15 minutes

Cook Time: 20 minutes

Difficulty: Moderate

Ingredients:

- ✓ 200g flat rice noodles

- ✓ 400g pork tenderloin, boiled and thinly sliced

- ✓ 1 red bell pepper, julienned & 2 spring onions, sliced

- ✓ 2 cloves garlic, minced & 2 tbsp soy sauce

- ✓ 1 tbsp fish sauce & 1 tsp brown sugar

- ✓ 1 tbsp vegetable oil
- ✓ Fresh cilantro and crushed peanuts for garnish

Step-by-Step Preparation:

1. Cook the rice noodles as per the package instructions and set aside.
2. In a pan, heat vegetable oil and sauté garlic until fragrant.
3. Add sliced pork, bell pepper, and spring onions, stir-frying for a few minutes.
4. Mix in the soy sauce, fish sauce, and brown sugar. Stir well.
5. Add the cooked noodles, and toss to combine.
6. Serve hot, garnished with fresh cilantro and crushed peanuts.

Nutritional Facts: (Per serving)

- ➢ Calories: 380 kcal
- ➢ Protein: 28g
- ➢ Carbohydrates: 40g
- ➢ Dietary Fiber: 2g
- ➢ Sugars: 3g
- ➢ Fat: 10g
- ➢ Sodium: 700mg

With "Thai Noodles with Boiled Pork," you're not just savoring a dish but experiencing a delightful blend of Thai authenticity and high-protein goodness. This veggie-twist masterpiece is comforting and refreshingly light, making it perfect for any mealtime occasion.

Recipe 90: Mushrooms Stuffed with Spinach

Savor the delightful combination of earthy mushrooms and nutritious spinach with "Mushrooms Stuffed with Spinach." This high-protein veggie-twist recipe is a tantalizing treat that's perfect as an appetizer or a light meal, offering rich flavors in every bite.

Servings: 4

Prepping Time: 15 minutes

Cook Time: 20 minutes

Difficulty: Easy

Ingredients:

- 8 large button mushrooms, stems removed

- 2 cups fresh spinach, chopped & 1/2 cup feta cheese, crumbled

- 2 cloves garlic, minced

- 1 tbsp olive oil

- Salt and pepper, to taste
- 1/4 cup grated parmesan cheese for topping

Step-by-Step Preparation:

1. Preheat the oven to 375°F (190°C).
2. In a pan, heat olive oil and sauté garlic until fragrant.
3. Add spinach and cook until wilted. Season with salt and pepper.
4. Remove from heat and mix in feta cheese.
5. Stuff each mushroom cap with the spinach mixture.
6. Place stuffed mushrooms on a baking tray and sprinkle with parmesan cheese.
7. Bake for 20 minutes or until mushrooms are tender and the cheese is golden.

Nutritional Facts: (Per serving)

- Calories: 110 kcal
- Protein: 7g
- Carbohydrates: 4g
- Dietary Fiber: 1g
- Sugars: 2g
- Fat: 8g
- Sodium: 210mg

Experience the joy of dining with "Mushrooms Stuffed with Spinach," an indulgent and nourishing dish. This veggie-twist delicacy ensures every forkful is a burst of flavor and health, making it a must-try for all food enthusiasts.

Chapter 10: Plant Protein Winners

Recipe 91: Chinese Dish from Chaozhou

Dive into the rich culinary tradition of Chaozhou with this authentic "Chinese Dish from Chaozhou." A perfect blend of flavors and plant proteins, this dish combines the best Chinese cuisine in a healthy and delicious way, ideal for vegans and vegetarians.

Servings: 4

Prepping Time: 20 minutes

Cook Time: 30 minutes

Difficulty: Moderate

Ingredients:

- ✓ 1 cup tofu, cubed
- ✓ 2 cups bock choy, chopped
- ✓ 1/2 cup shiitake mushrooms, sliced
- ✓ 2 cloves garlic, minced

- ✓ 2 tbsp soy sauce
- ✓ 1 tsp sesame oil
- ✓ 1/2 tsp white pepper
- ✓ 2 green onions, chopped
- ✓ 1 tbsp ginger, finely chopped

Step-by-Step Preparation:

1. Heat sesame oil in a wok over medium heat.
2. Add garlic and ginger, and sauté until fragrant.
3. Incorporate tofu and shiitake mushrooms, cooking until lightly browned.
4. Stir in bock choy, soy sauce, and white pepper.
5. Cook until bock choy wilts and ingredients are well mixed.
6. Garnish with green onions before serving.

Nutritional Facts: (Per serving)

- ➢ Calories: 90 kcal
- ➢ Protein: 8g
- ➢ Carbohydrates: 6g
- ➢ Dietary Fiber: 2g
- ➢ Sugars: 2g
- ➢ Fat: 4g
- ➢ Sodium: 420mg

Embark on a delightful gastronomic journey with the "Chinese Dish from Chaozhou." This Plant Protein Winner ensures that you're not just enjoying a meal but also embracing the cultural richness of Chinese culinary traditions while nourishing your body.

Recipe 92: Vegan Fried Teriyaki Tofu

Satisfy your taste buds with "Vegan Fried Teriyaki Tofu," a compelling fusion of crispy tofu drenched in savory teriyaki. A delicious testimony to plant-based wonders, this dish will leave you craving more while loading you with pure plant protein.

Servings: 4

Prepping Time: 15 minutes

Cook Time: 20 minutes

Difficulty: Easy

Ingredients:

- ✓ 1 block of firm tofu, pressed and cubed
- ✓ 3 tbsp soy sauce
- ✓ 2 tbsp maple syrup or agave nectar
- ✓ 1 tbsp rice vinegar
- ✓ 1 tsp grated ginger

- ✓ 2 cloves garlic, minced
- ✓ 1 tbsp sesame oil
- ✓ 2 tbsp cornstarch
- ✓ Green onions and sesame seeds for garnish

Step-by-Step Preparation:

1. Mix soy sauce, maple syrup, rice vinegar, ginger, and garlic in a bowl to create the teriyaki sauce.

2. Toss tofu cubes in cornstarch to coat evenly.

3. Heat sesame oil in a skillet and fry tofu until golden.

4. Pour the teriyaki sauce over the tofu and simmer until the sauce thickens.

5. Garnish with green onions and sesame seeds before serving.

Nutritional Facts: (Per serving)

- ➢ Calories: 190 kcal
- ➢ Protein: 12g
- ➢ Carbohydrates: 18g
- ➢ Dietary Fiber: 1g
- ➢ Sugars: 10g
- ➢ Fat: 8g
- ➢ Sodium: 850mg

Dive into a plate of "Vegan Fried Teriyaki Tofu" as a testament to the power of plant-based cuisine and as a delicious treat that packs flavor and nutrition in every bite. This Plant Protein Winner is sure to be a hit at any mealtime.

Recipe 93: Vegan Grilled Vegetables

Unearth the elegance of simple flavors with "Vegan Grilled Vegetables." Revel in the charred goodness of seasonal veggies as they intertwine with fragrant herbs, presenting a plate full of nourishing plant protein and nature's vibrant colors.

Servings: 4

Prepping Time: 15 minutes

Cook Time: 20 minutes

Difficulty: Easy

Ingredients:

- ✓ 2 zucchinis, sliced
- ✓ 1 red bell pepper, cut into strips
- ✓ 1 yellow bell pepper, cut into strips
- ✓ 1 large eggplant, sliced
- ✓ 2 tbsp olive oil
- ✓ 1 tbsp balsamic vinegar
- ✓ Salt and pepper, to taste
- ✓ Fresh herbs (like rosemary or thyme) for garnish

Step-by-Step Preparation:

1. Preheat the grill to medium-high.

2. Drizzle olive oil and balsamic vinegar over the vegetables.

3. Season with salt, pepper, and any preferred herbs.

4. Grill the vegetables until charred and tender, turning occasionally.

5. Garnish with fresh herbs before serving.

Nutritional Facts: (Per serving)

- Calories: 110 kcal

- Protein: 3g

- Carbohydrates: 14g

- Dietary Fiber: 5g

- Sugars: 8g

- Fat: 5g

- Sodium: 10mg

Relish the simplicity and wholesomeness of "Vegan Grilled Vegetables," where every bite takes you on a journey through nature's bountiful garden. This Plant Protein Winner epitomizes how delicious and nutritious vegan cuisine can be.

Recipe 94: Teriyaki Tofu Salad

Dive into the delightful fusion of crispy tofu glazed with teriyaki and fresh, crunchy greens. "Teriyaki Tofu Salad" is a feast for the eyes and a nutrient-packed culinary experience celebrating plant protein at its finest.

Servings: 4

Prepping Time: 20 minutes

Cook Time: 15 minutes

Difficulty: Moderate

Ingredients:

- ✓ 400g firm tofu, cubed
- ✓ 4 tbsp teriyaki sauce
- ✓ 1 tbsp sesame oil
- ✓ 2 cups mixed salad greens
- ✓ 1 red bell pepper, thinly sliced
- ✓ 1 cucumber, sliced

- ✓ 2 green onions, chopped
- ✓ 1 tbsp toasted sesame seeds

Step-by-Step Preparation:

1. Press tofu to remove excess water and then cube.

2. Heat sesame oil in a pan and add tofu cubes, frying until golden brown.

3. Glaze tofu with teriyaki sauce and cook until it's caramelized.

4. Combine salad greens, bell pepper, cucumber, and green onions in a bowl.

5. Top the salad with teriyaki tofu and sprinkle sesame seeds.

Nutritional Facts: (Per serving)

- ➤ Calories: 210 kcal
- ➤ Protein: 13g
- ➤ Carbohydrates: 16g
- ➤ Dietary Fiber: 2g
- ➤ Sugars: 10g
- ➤ Fat: 10g
- ➤ Sodium: 550mg

Relish the harmonious blend of savory teriyaki tofu with the refreshing crunch of assorted veggies. "Teriyaki Tofu Salad" is the epitome of how plant-based meals can be both tantalizingly delicious and rich in protein.

Recipe 95: Vegan Breakfast Prepared

Start your day with an energizing burst of plant-based goodness. "Vegan Breakfast Prepared" is a curated ensemble of flavors and nutrients designed to kickstart your morning, ensuring you're fueled and ready for the day ahead.

Servings: 4

Prepping Time: 15 minutes

Cook Time: 20 minutes

Difficulty: Easy

Ingredients:

- ✓ 1 cup quinoa, rinsed
- ✓ 2 tbsp almond butter
- ✓ 1 tbsp chia seeds
- ✓ 1/2 cup almond milk
- ✓ 1 cup mixed berries

- ✓ 1/4 cup crushed walnuts
- ✓ 2 tbsp maple syrup
- ✓ 1 tsp vanilla extract

Step-by-Step Preparation:

1. Cook quinoa as per package instructions.
2. Combine almond butter, chia seeds, almond milk, maple syrup, and vanilla extract in a mixing bowl.
3. Mix in cooked quinoa until well combined.
4. Serve in bowls, topping with mixed berries and crushed walnuts.

Nutritional Facts: (Per serving)

- ➤ Calories: 280 kcal
- ➤ Protein: 8g
- ➤ Carbohydrates: 45g
- ➤ Dietary Fiber: 7g
- ➤ Sugars: 15g
- ➤ Fat: 10g
- ➤ Sodium: 10mg

Indulge in a morning meal that's as delightful to the taste buds as it benefits your health. "Vegan Breakfast Prepared" perfectly represents how a plant-based start can pave the way for a day full of energy and zest.

Recipe 96: Fresh Vietnamese Spring Rolls

Delve into the refreshing world of Vietnamese cuisine with these "Fresh Vietnamese Spring Rolls." Each roll is a harmony of textures and flavors, beautifully encased in delicate rice paper.

Servings: 4

Prepping Time: 20 minutes

Cook Time: 5 minutes

Difficulty: Intermediate

Ingredients:

- ✓ 8 rice paper sheets
- ✓ 1 cup firm tofu, thinly sliced
- ✓ 1 cup lettuce, shredded
- ✓ 1/2 cup mint leaves
- ✓ 1/2 cup cilantro leaves
- ✓ 1 carrot, julienned

✓ 1 cucumber, julienned

✓ 1/2 cup rice noodles, cooked

Step-by-Step Preparation:

1. Soften rice paper sheets by dipping them in warm water for a few seconds.

2. Lay flat on a work surface and place a bit of each ingredient in the center.

3. Fold the sides over the filling, then roll up tightly.

4. Repeat with the remaining ingredients.

5. Serve with a dipping sauce of your choice.

Nutritional Facts: (Per serving)

➢ Calories: 150 kcal

➢ Protein: 6g

➢ Carbohydrates: 26g

➢ Dietary Fiber: 2g

➢ Sugars: 3g

➢ Fat: 3g

➢ Sodium: 15mg

Add a burst of freshness to your meals with these Vietnamese Spring Rolls. Perfect for a light lunch or as an appetizer, they encapsulate the essence of plant-based nutrition and authentic Southeast Asian flavors.

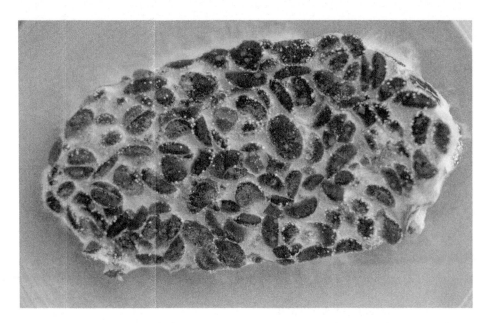

Recipe 97: Tempeh is a Soy-Based Food

Discover the delightful world of tempeh, a renowned soy-based superfood. This versatile ingredient, native to Indonesia, is celebrated for its rich, nutty flavor and unparalleled nutritional profile. Dive into a delectable dish that champions tempeh's unique charm.

Servings: 4

Prepping Time: 15 minutes

Cook Time: 20 minutes

Difficulty: Easy

Ingredients:

- ✓ 200g tempeh, sliced
- ✓ 2 tbsp soy sauce
- ✓ 1 tbsp sesame oil
- ✓ 2 garlic cloves, minced
- ✓ 1 tsp ginger, grated

- ✓ 1 tbsp maple syrup
- ✓ 1 red bell pepper, sliced
- ✓ 2 green onions, chopped

Step-by-Step Preparation:

1. Mix soy sauce, sesame oil, garlic, ginger, and maple syrup in a bowl.
2. Marinate tempeh slices in the mixture for 10 minutes.
3. Heat a skillet and cook tempeh until browned on each side.
4. Add red bell pepper slices and cook until soft.
5. Garnish with green onions before serving.

Nutritional Facts: (Per serving)

- ➤ Calories: 170 kcal
- ➤ Protein: 13g
- ➤ Carbohydrates: 10g
- ➤ Dietary Fiber: 2g
- ➤ Sugars: 6g
- ➤ Fat: 9g
- ➤ Sodium: 550mg

Experience the wholesome goodness of tempeh in this simple yet delicious preparation. An ideal choice for those venturing into plant-based diets, tempeh is truly a testament to nature's nutritious bounty.

Recipe 98: Buddha Bowl of Mixed Vegetables

Embrace a holistic dining experience with the Buddha Bowl of Mixed Vegetables. A colorful medley of fresh produce and hearty grains, this dish is a testament to plant-based perfection, offering nutrition and indulgence in every bite.

Servings: 4

Prepping Time: 20 minutes

Cook Time: 25 minutes

Difficulty: Easy

Ingredients:

- ✓ 1 cup quinoa, rinsed and drained
- ✓ 2 cups mixed vegetables (broccoli, bell peppers, carrots)
- ✓ 1 cup chickpeas, drained and rinsed & 1 avocado, sliced
- ✓ 2 tbsp olive oil & Salt and pepper to taste

✓ 1 tbsp sesame seeds & 2 tbsp tahini sauce

Step-by-Step Preparation:

1. Cook quinoa according to package instructions.

2. On a baking tray, spread mixed vegetables, drizzle with olive oil, season with salt and pepper, and roast at 400°F for 20 minutes.

3. Add cooked quinoa, roasted vegetables, chickpeas, and avocado slices to serve bowls.

4. Drizzle with tahini sauce and sprinkle with sesame seeds.

Nutritional Facts: (Per serving)

➢ Calories: 320 kcal

➢ Protein: 12g

➢ Carbohydrates: 45g

➢ Dietary Fiber: 10g

➢ Sugars: 5g

➢ Fat: 12g

➢ Sodium: 150mg

Delve into this Buddha Bowl's harmonious blend of flavors and textures. It's not just a meal; it's a celebration of the plant kingdom's vibrant and nourishing offerings. Every spoonful promises a journey of well-being.

Recipe 99: Tacos with a Salad of Vegetables

Savor the vibrant fusion of flavors in these Tacos with a Salad of Vegetables. This dish is a testament to how nourishing and delightful plant-based meals can be, giving your taste buds and body a treat.

Servings: 4

Prepping Time: 20 minutes

Cook Time: 15 minutes

Difficulty: Easy

Ingredients:

- ✓ 8 small corn tortillas
- ✓ 2 cups mixed beans (black, kidney, and chickpeas), cooked
- ✓ 1 large bell pepper, sliced & 1 cup cherry tomatoes, halved
- ✓ 1 cucumber, diced & 1 avocado, sliced
- ✓ 1/4 cup fresh cilantro, chopped & 1 lime, juiced
- ✓ 2 tbsp olive oil & Salt and pepper, to taste
- ✓ 1 tsp ground cumin &1 tsp chili powder

Step-by-Step Preparation:

1. Combine beans, bell pepper, cherry tomatoes, and cucumber in a large bowl.

2. Whisk together lime juice, olive oil, cumin, chili powder, salt, and pepper in a separate bowl to create the dressing.

3. Pour the sauce over the vegetable and bean mix, tossing gently to coat.

4. Heat tortillas in a skillet over medium heat until slightly charred.

5. Divide the salad mix among tortillas, garnish with avocado slices and cilantro.

6. Serve immediately and enjoy!

Nutritional Facts: (Per serving)

- Calories: 350

- Protein: 12g

- Carbohydrates: 48g

- Dietary Fiber: 10g

- Sugars: 5g

- Fat: 14g

- Saturated Fat: 2g

- Sodium: 250mg

Unleash the power of plant protein with these invigorating tacos, offering not just a burst of flavors but also a cascade of nutrients. Perfect for those seeking wholesome yet delicious meals, this dish promises to become a staple in your culinary repertoire. Cheers to healthy eating!

Recipe 100: A Yellow Veg Thai Curry with Tofu

Indulge in the rich and aromatic flavors of this Yellow Veg Thai Curry with Tofu. With its creamy consistency and hearty tofu chunks, this vegan delight seamlessly marries nutrition and taste, making every spoonful an adventure for the senses.

Servings: 4

Prepping Time: 25 minutes

Cook Time: 20 minutes

Difficulty: Intermediate

Ingredients:

- ✓ 200g firm tofu, cubed & 2 cups coconut milk

- ✓ 2 tbsp yellow curry paste & 1 red bell pepper, sliced

- ✓ 1 zucchini, sliced & 1 carrot, sliced

- ✓ 2 cloves garlic, minced & 1 onion, chopped

- ✓ 1 tbsp soy sauce & 1 tsp brown sugar
- ✓ Fresh basil leaves for garnish & 2 tbsp vegetable oil & Salt, to taste

Step-by-Step Preparation:

1. Heat vegetable oil in a pan and sauté onions and garlic until translucent.

2. Add yellow curry paste, stir well, and cook for 2 minutes.

3. Incorporate coconut milk, soy sauce, and brown sugar, bringing to a gentle simmer.

4. Add bell pepper, zucchini, and carrot, cooking until vegetables are tender.

5. Introduce tofu cubes, simmering for another 5-7 minutes.

6. Adjust seasoning with salt.

7. Serve hot, garnished with fresh basil leaves.

Nutritional Facts: (Per serving)

- ➢ Calories: 320
- ➢ Protein: 12g
- ➢ Carbohydrates: 16g
- ➢ Dietary Fiber: 4g
- ➢ Sugars: 6g
- ➢ Fat: 24g
- ➢ Saturated Fat: 19g
- ➢ Sodium: 370mg

Let this Yellow Veg Thai Curry with Tofu transport you to the streets of Thailand, allowing you to relish authentic flavors in the comfort of your home. A plant-protein-packed dish that doesn't skimp on taste, it's proof that vegan meals can indeed be rich, creamy, and utterly irresistible.

Conclusion

Conclusion for "Healthy High-Protein Air Fryer Recipes Stunning 100 Photos: Delicious & Original Ideas for Every Dish!" by Oliver Brentwood

Food lovers, health enthusiasts, and culinary explorers, we've embarked on an extraordinary journey through the world of high-protein delights, all the while unlocking the potential of our trusty air fryer.

From the crispy edges of tender chicken to the fluffy core of protein-packed pancakes, Oliver Brentwood has served up a symphony of flavors in **"Healthy High-Protein Air Fryer Recipes Stunning 100 Photos."** The recipes have been about satiating our hunger and introducing a healthier way of living without compromising on taste. With each page turned, we've been tormented by vibrant photographs that have ignited our senses and beckoned us to our kitchens.

But what truly sets this book apart is its commitment to originality. Oliver doesn't just rehash old recipes with minor tweaks; he ventures into culinary realms few have trodden. Whether you're a seasoned chef or a novice just beginning to explore the depths of your air fryer, this book has presented something new and exciting for everyone. The balance between health and flavor, the meticulous detail, and the passion evident in every recipe have set a new standard for air fryer cookbooks.

So, as we reach the end of our journey, let it not be the end of yours. Use this book as your trusty guide, your companion in the kitchen. Try a new recipe every week, introduce friends and family to the wonders of healthy air-fried cuisine, and above all, keep the spirit of culinary exploration alive. **Oliver Brentwood's** masterpiece isn't just a collection of recipes; it's an invitation to a healthier, tastier future.